BLACKSTONE'S
PREPARING FOR POLICE DUTY

BLACKSTONE'S
PREPARING FOR
POLICE DUTY

Fourth Edition

Richard Butterworth and
Fraser Sampson

OXFORD
UNIVERSITY PRESS

OXFORD

UNIVERSITY PRESS

Great Clarendon Street, Oxford OX2 6DP

Oxford University Press is a department of the University of Oxford.
It furthers the University's objective of excellence in research, scholarship,
and education by publishing worldwide in

Oxford New York

Auckland Cape Town Dar es Salaam Hong Kong Karachi
Kuala Lumpur Madrid Melbourne Mexico City Nairobi
New Delhi Shanghai Taipei Toronto

With offices in

Argentina Austria Brazil Chile Czech Republic France Greece
Guatemala Hungary Italy Japan Poland Portugal Singapore
South Korea Switzerland Thailand Turkey Ukraine Vietnam

Oxford is a registered trade mark of Oxford University Press
in the UK and in certain other countries

Published in the United States
by Oxford University Press Inc., New York

First published 2003
Fourth edition published 2010

British Library Cataloguing-in-Publication Data

Data available

Library of Congress Cataloging-in-Publication Data

Butterworth, Richard.
    Blackstone's preparing for police duty.—4th ed. / Richard Butterworth, Fraser Sampson.
    p. cm.
    Rev. ed. of: Blackstone's preparing for police duty / Phil Hardy and Fraser Sampson. 3rd ed. 2008.
    ISBN 978-0-19-959523-5 (pbk.)
    1. Police recruits—England—Handbooks, manuals, etc. 2. Police recruits—Wales—Handbooks,
manuals, etc. 3. Police training—England. 4. Police training—Wales. 5. Police—England.
6. Police—Wales. I. Sampson, Fraser. II. Hardy, Phil. Blackstone's preparing for police duty.
III. Title. IV. Title: Preparing for police duty.
    HV8196.A2S35 2010
    363.220942—dc22   2010032987

Typeset by Glyph International, Bangalore, India
Printed in Great Britain
on acid-free paper by
CPI Antony Rowe, Chippenham, Wiltshire

ISBN 978-0-19-959523-5

10 9 8 7 6 5 4 3 2 1

Foreword: Preparing for Police Duty

For over thirty years I have been proud to serve as an officer in various forces throughout the country. Over this time I have seen a staggering amount of change within the police service as new challenges have been met and officer professionalism and support have been improved. Being a police officer remains an exciting and rewarding career choice, but no one should forget that it is a demanding and difficult role that requires a great deal of dedication and hard work to meet the high expectations of the public.

Counter-terrorism, neighbourhood policing and new forms of crime have provided the impetus for the Service to transform itself and expand the workforce across the police family, but we should always remember that our core objectives and values remain unaltered since the inception of the police service nearly two centuries ago.

'Preparing for Police Duty' gives a comprehensive and valuable insight into the reality of what it means to be an officer in a modern day police force, as well as the legal and organisational structures that we operate within.

It is an excellent reference for anyone wishing to gain a wider under-standing of the police service and the role and responsibilities it has within society.

Meredydd Hughes, QPM
Chief Constable
South Yorkshire Police

Foreword: Preparing for Duty

I am very pleased as the representative of police authorities, working on behalf of local communities across England, Wales and Northern Ireland, to contribute a Foreword to this book, which is without doubt essential reading for those about to enter today's policing world.

Police authorities work independently, on behalf of local people, to hold Chief Constables (Commissioners in London) to account for policing in their local areas. We listen to communities in order to put them at the heart of policing, whilst our police authority members work at both local and national levels to ensure that local voices influence policing.

The police service has made great strides in listening to what people want from it and there is growing recognition of the importance of effective local connections. But the police service needs to do much more than listen to communities. Working with police authorities, I believe the service must always be seen to act according to local community needs, whilst ensuring that ways of developing an enhanced dialogue with local people are continuously improved.

Preparing for duty is without doubt an incredibly important undertaking for all police officers. On behalf of the communities you will serve I wish you well in this task, and in your future career, in this most critical of public services.

Rob Garnham
Chair, Association of Police Authorities

Acknowledgements

Like the endeavours of all good teams, writing a book relies on a great deal of support from many people and I would like to thank just a few. First, to my wife Kelly, a serving police sergeant, and children Emma, Chloe and Oliver for bearing with me when glued to the laptop late into the night.

Many thanks to Phil Hardy for his work on the third edition of this book, which was a tremendous achievement and success.

I am also grateful to Katie and Peter at Oxford University Press for their support, guidance and assistance with the book and for their encouragement throughout.

But the biggest thanks must go to the job I love and to the many colleagues I have worked with at both West and South Yorkshire Police and forces around the country.

Policing is not for the fainthearted. In my service I have been shot at by an armed suspect and endured a 24-hour tour of duty being on the frontline of the largest riot and worst public disorder in the north of England in recent memory, where over 400 police officers were injured. I am forever mindful of the courageous acts and minor miracles performed by officers on a daily basis, as well as the bravery they show and the selfless sacrifices they make. As always it is down to the sheer enthusiasm of colleagues, who frequently go above and beyond the call of duty, to help those in need in cities, towns and villages throughout the country. This one's for you.

Richard Butterworth

About the Authors

Richard Butterworth

Chief Inspector Richard Butterworth has 15 years' policing experience and was born and brought up near Halifax, West Yorkshire. After graduating from Goldsmiths' College, University of London, he considered careers as an army officer and as a journalist before joining West Yorkshire Police and being posted to Huddersfield.

Having worked in many departments, including Response Policing, CID, Intelligence, Custody and the Firearms Support Unit, he was also trained as a Public Order Tactical Adviser and has been awarded several District Commander and Chief Officer commendations. He also acted as an assistant spotter for Huddersfield Town AFC, which meant travelling around the country and taking part in many large football operations. He was also a force liaison for a local volunteer search and rescue team.

Whilst a Sergeant, he led countless firearms operations throughout the West Yorkshire area, which involved facing some extremely dangerous and challenging situations. Upon transferring to South Yorkshire Police as an Inspector, he led frontline policing teams across Sheffield, as well as having a role as a public order commander.

As a Chief Inspector and staff officer to the Chief Constable, he has been involved in national planning for the London 2012 Olympic Games, the Papal Visit 2010 and writing guidance on behalf of the ACPO Uniformed Operations Business Area. He continues to have a role in operational work and is a football and CBRN commander.

He lives with his family in a small village situated on the West and South Yorkshire border and still enjoys turning his arm for a local cricket team.

Fraser Sampson

Fraser Sampson LL.B., LL.M., MBA is Chief Executive and Solicitor of the West Yorkshire Police Authority. Formerly head of National Police Training Examinations and Assessment, he has written and edited a number of leading police titles for Oxford University Press and has represented police officers in a range of legal proceedings. He is a Visiting Fellow at the University of Glamorgan, an International Fellow of the JAMS Foundation in the US and an advisory board member of the Centre for Criminal Justice Studies at Leeds University.

Fraser was the author of the first edition of Blackstone's *Preparing for Police Duty.*

Contents

CONTENTS

Introduction

As an outsider looking in, policing seems like a straightforward business; catching criminals, keeping people and communities safe and being on hand to respond to emergencies when required by the public. All these things are true, and doubtless will remain at the heart of what the police do and how they do it.

But, as this book will detail, policing is a complicated business—and it is getting more complicated all the time. Over the past ten years, policing within England and Wales has changed dramatically and will change even further over the next decade; yet police officers will still be there to deal with all the incidents mentioned above, and more.

Some of the changes have been in response to new legislation and new police powers. Other changes have been in response to changing public attitudes and expectations as to how communities wish to be policed and the services they demand.

How the police service responds to these changes has been critical to ensuring that it remains an organisation that the public can trust and have confidence in, to solve their problems and be there when needed.

Some things will never change, such as frequent news headlines about the police and crime related matters. It is testament to the society we live in that the police service is something that any member of the community can make a contribution towards and have a stake in. Policing can have such an impact on our lives that it has become one of the key elements determining quality of life within a regional, community or even a family setting.

There is no such thing as an easy policing job. As well as the key motivational factors, physical attributes and potential for development, effective, efficient and professional policing requires effective, efficient and professional training.

So if you are considering a career in the police, or have been through the recruit assessment process or are undergoing training in a support or auxiliary role, this book is intended to help you.

There are limits on the depth and breadth that can be covered in a book of this nature, but the content has been designed to show what policing is really like for the front-line officer and to unravel some of the mysteries of preparing for police duty.

As of August 2010, it is likely that the tripartite system will change over the next few years, with the government outlining its intention to abolish police authorities, and replace them with locally elected Police and Crime Commissioners (except in the Metropolitan Police area). Although the date set for this transition is 2012, it is likely that the role of a Commissioner will focus upon setting priorities and being held accountable to the public for policing delivery and performance in their area. This is likely to lead to a shift in the relationship with local Chief Constables; as it is clear that Commissioners will have additional involvement in examining operational policing, whilst linking this closely to overall performance and value for money.

The public and senior officers will be equally keen to assess the proposed developments and the effects they will have upon policing services within communities. Such changes, and the ever-growing appetite for additional accountability, will be an interesting move and one that will be sure to shape the policing landscape for years to come.

The government has also stated that they wish to disestablish the National Policing Improvement Agency (NPIA) within the same period and to hand many responsibilities back to forces, although the precise details of this move have yet to be finalised.

PART I

THE POLICE

1

IN THE OFFICE OF CONSTABLE

I .... of .... do solemnly and sincerely declare and affirm that I will well and truly serve the Queen in the office of constable with fairness, integrity, diligence and impartiality, upholding fundamental human rights and according equal respect to all people; and that I will, to the best of my power, cause the peace to be kept and preserved and prevent all offences against people and property; and that while I continue to hold the said office, I will, to the best of my skill and knowledge, discharge all the duties thereof faithfully according to law.

I.I The Office of Constable

The office of constable can be traced back as far as the 14th century and the idea of a local person taking an oath in front of a magistrate to keep the peace and enforce the law and, as a result, being given special powers over their fellow citizens.

The fact that the office of constable is still in use is the legal source of every police officer's powers and defines the duties and responsibilities that go hand in hand with those powers. Every police officer in the country from the newest recruit through to the Chief Constables who head the individual police forces in England and Wales are constables, first and foremost.

As a constable you are not an employee and do not generally have a contract of employment (though officers in forces such as the British Transport Police and Civil Nuclear Constabulary do). The force you join will pay you and direct your work, but it is not because you work for your force that you will have the—limited—powers to stop, search, arrest and so forth. It is because you hold the office of constable, and when you exercise those powers you are personally responsible for the actions you take and the way you take them.

Your life, on duty and off, will be governed by police regulations and the code of conduct. We will look at this in detail later, but it is worth exploring their effects a little here.

1.2 The Effect on Your Private Life

If you are going to be a police officer your integrity, honesty and impartiality must be beyond question. To this end there are certain restrictions on what officers can do in their private lives as well as when they are at work. For example, you will not be able to belong to certain organisations or go on strike. These are some of the explicit restrictions that you will have to live with, but probably the bigger impact is the implicit restrictions that come with 'The Job'.

Once you are a police officer people will look at you differently. Your neighbours, acquaintances, even friends and, perhaps, family will know what you do for a living and look at how you live your life accordingly. They will expect certain things of you.

From now on when there is a problem, a car crash, a disturbance, a serious crime, a major disaster, when all the public are moving away from the scene, as a police officer you are the one who is heading in the other direction. You are the one who is going to deal with it. It is what the public expects, it is what you get paid for, it is 'The Job'.

1.3 Respect and Accountability

Let us just look at the attestation again for a moment. 'Fairness, integrity, diligence and impartiality', no problems there, it is what you would expect. How about 'according equal respect to all people'? Treating decent, honest, law-abiding people with respect, is that a problem? But it says 'all people'. That includes the person you have just arrested for raping a child. That includes the violent drunk who, after assaulting you, adds insult to injury by being sick down the front of your uniform. That includes the woman who, after the fourth time you have arrested her husband for beating her up, once again says she does not wish to support a prosecution. Treating everybody with equal respect, and not just the respect you may think they deserve, is not easy, but it is what you have to do once you hold the office of constable.

As a constable you will have powers above those granted to your fellow citizens. The powers you will have are also far wider than those given to any other group. They include the power to:

- arrest;
- stop people and vehicles;
- enter premises;
- search people, buildings and vehicles;
- seize property;
- issue fixed penalty fine notices;
- cordon off streets; and
- control and direct traffic.

There are, of course, restrictions on when and how you may exercise these powers, and each time you do so it is on your own judgement and your own responsibility. It is because you have such powers that the public, who entrusted you with them, demands that you are strictly accountable for the way in which you use them.

There is an awful lot of writing and administration involved in being a police officer. An incident or an arrest on the street that lasts only a few minutes can, and often does, generate several hours' worth of computer updating or paperwork. Most, if not all, police officers, of whatever rank, get frustrated by the amount of administration, but, just like having to verbally explain your actions under cross-examination in a court of law or other enquiry, it is the price that has to be paid for having the powers needed to police our modern society.

1.4 The Job

Restrictions on private life, always being on duty, having to deal with people at their worst regardless of personal feelings and then having to be able to justify in minute detail what you did, quite aside from the more obvious elements such as risk and personal danger; why do people do 'The Job'?

Well the phrase, 'The Job', itself gives a clue. There is great pride there; it is as if policing is the only job worth doing, and for many that's true. Certainly holding the office of constable will affect your whole life and offer enormous satisfaction in a way few, if any, other jobs can.

In this chapter you have seen that every police officer holds a public office, that of constable, which is the source of the powers they exercise and the responsibilities that they have. In the rest of this part of the book we will look at how policing in England and Wales is organised, structured and managed.

FURTHER READING

→ Sir Robert Mark, *In the Office of Constable*, 1978, HarperCollins.

2

HISTORY AND STRUCTURE
OF POLICING

The office of constable is an ancient one but the police service is a much more recent institution. The purpose of this chapter is to give you an understanding of how today's police service came to have the structure that it does.

2.1 Policing Reflects Society

Like all public services, the police service has undergone significant change, even in the last 10–15 years. This change has been difficult to adapt to, and at times difficult to achieve. But it is something that has been replicated in areas such as healthcare, teaching and local government.

Policing has always been changing; it has to because the society it is part of and serves has always been changing. The only thing that is different now is the pace of change.

2.2 The Beginning

The origins of modern policing date back to the late 18th century. This was a time of massive social change. The industrial revolution was in full swing and people were leaving the land in droves to seek work in the mills, mines and factories of the rapidly expanding towns and cities.

Such large-scale social change inevitably brought with it crime and disorder. By the 1780s it was clear that the existing system of parish constables, watchmen, and the few private police forces that then existed could not cope with the former, and after the Peterloo Massacre, where 11 people were killed and 400 injured, the old practice of using the Army to suppress civil disorder was no longer acceptable.

When Sir Robert Peel succeeded in getting the Metropolitan Police Act passed in 1829 the era of modern policing was born and the first full-time paid constables stepped onto the streets of central London in September of that year.

2.3 Peel's Nine Principles of Policing

As well as being successful in getting constables on the beat, Peel also defined the ethos of modern policing within his nine principles, which are just as relevant as today as when they were written over 180 years ago. They are:

1. To prevent crime and disorder, as an alternative to their repression by military force and by severity of legal punishment.
2. To recognise always that the power of the police to fulfil their functions and duties is dependent on public approval of their existence, actions and behaviour, and on their ability to secure and maintain public respect.
3. To recognise always that to secure and maintain the respect and approval of the public means also the securing of willing cooperation of the public in the task of securing observance of laws.
4. To recognise always that the extent to which the cooperation of the public can be secured diminishes, proportionately, the necessity of the use of physical force and compulsion for achieving police objectives.
5. To seek and to preserve public favour, not by pandering to public opinion, but by constantly demonstrating absolutely impartial service to law, in complete independence of policy, and without regard to

the justice or injustices of the substance of individual laws; by ready offering of individual services and friendship to all members of the public without regard to their wealth or social standing; by ready exercise of courtesy and friendly good humour; and by ready offering of individual sacrifice in protecting and preserving life.

6. To use physical force only when the exercise of persuasion, advice and warning is found insufficient to obtain public cooperation to an extent necessary to secure observance of law or to restore order; and to use only the minimum degree of physical force which is necessary on any particular occasion for achieving a police objective.

7. To maintain at all times a relationship with the public that gives reality to the historic tradition that the police are the public and the public are the police; the police being only members of the public who are paid to give full-time attention to duties which are incumbent on every citizen, in the interests of community, welfare and existence.

8. To recognise always the need for strict adherence to police-executive functions, and to refrain from even seeming to usurp the powers of the judiciary of avenging individuals or the State, and of authoritatively judging guilt and punishing the guilty.

9. To recognise always that the test of police efficiency is the absence of crime and disorder, and not the visible evidence of police action in dealing with them.

Peel set a new model of policing, one that suited the English social and political temperament and one that still guides the Service of today and was referred to recently in the HMIC report 'Adapting to Protest—Nurturing the British model of Policing' (2009) as the most essential and relevant aspiration of the police service.

2.4 **The New Police**

After a shaky start, the Metropolitan Police soon became an accepted, popular and successful institution.

In response to rising crime rates, the Town and County Police Act 1856 was passed. This Act required all counties, large towns and cities to set up their own police forces. In effect, this Act laid the foundation stone for the unique tripartite system of police management that we have today. We will look in detail at how this operates in Chapter 3; for now it is only necessary to note the three bodies and their main respective responsibilities.

- The Home Office—responsible for policing in general, the maintenance of national standards and paying (in most cases) the majority of the costs.
- Local Police Authorities—responsible for providing and maintaining an efficient and effective force for their area, holding the Chief Constable/ Commissioner to account and paying a percentage of policing costs (raised through local taxes).
- The Chief Constable (Commissioner in the Metropolitan and City of London forces)—responsible for the operations of their force.

The model of police organisation set up by the 1856 Act may be recognisable to us today, but it certainly wasn't the last time that social pressures have caused the police to change accordingly. The major milestones and changes can be summarised as follows.

1920s—As the country recovered from World War I it was clear that the fundamental nature of society in England and Wales had changed. Reflecting this, the Desborough Committee aimed to make policing a profession and for the first time it was possible to appoint Chief Constables from officers who had risen through the ranks.

1946—During World War II the police in England and Wales were taken under direct Home Office control and grouped into Regional Commands. In addition, central government grants became a much bigger component of the funding of local authorities. The end of the war did not see the complete reversal of measures created to cope with the national emergency. Indeed society moved to a far more centralised and activist system of government. This centralising trend was reflected in the fact that the number of police forces was reduced to 119, with far more shared services such as training, laboratory and scientific facilities funded from the centre.

1960s—A series of scandals involving senior officers plus the advent of a more mobile and prosperous society led to the Royal Commission of 1960 and the resulting Police Act 1964. This saw the number of forces reduced again and the creation of the modern police authorities. After the 1964 Act and the reorganisation of local government in the early 1970s the number of forces was reduced to the current 43. The growing problem of criminals working across force borders was also recognised at this time, and to combat it six Regional Crime Squads staffed by detectives seconded from the local forces were set up.

1980s—In the early 1980s society was rocked by a series of riots in inner city areas (primarily Brixton and Tottenham in London, Toxteth in Liverpool, Handsworth in Birmingham and St Pauls in Bristol). The full causes of these large scale disturbances were complex and are beyond the scope of this book, but one large factor was the fact that policing had become divorced from the society it existed to protect and serve. After several inner city riots throughout the country the Service had to accept that it was now policing a multi-cultural society and needed to adapt and change accordingly, a process that continues to this day.

No discussion of changes to policing in the 1980s can be complete without mentioning the Police and Criminal Evidence Act 1984, known as PACE. A series of well publicised cases in which police powers were perceived to have been misused led to the Act, which radically reformed the way the Service carried out its business. The three big changes brought in were the introduction of national, well defined and limited powers to stop and search people (these had previously been available only to officers in some large cities); the tightening of the procedures when someone was arrested (including the universal provision of solicitors before and during interview); and the separation of investigation from prosecution (something that is only now coming to complete fruition). This was another example of policing having to change to keep pace with the demands of society.

1990s—One of the major themes that dominated many of the changes throughout the 1990s was the rise of the performance culture. Public concern over rising crime rates led to forces across the country being held more accountable for initiatives to tackle headline issues, such as burglary, robbery and car crime. This drive had effects on all levels of the Service, not just at senior management levels. Officers were increasingly required to deliver results and measured upon their overall performance, in areas such as arrests, intelligence submissions, and stop and searches. This rise of the performance culture within the Service was not without its critics, from both officers and policing commentators, but its influence upon many of the structures within forces can still be seen to this day.

2000 to present—After the attacks on New York in 2001 and on London in 2005, terrorism became a major theme for the Service with efforts not only to detect and disrupt the activities of terror groups, but also to work with communities to prevent people being drawn towards such activities in the first place. This has been a core theme of the Government's anti-terror strategy, which has seen considerable funds and resources being directed to this issue.

The 'Policing Pledge' was signed by all forces in 2009 and sets key standards around the delivery of policing services to the public in areas such as response times to emergencies and local consultation.

How the Service approached and dealt with the complexities of modern-day protest was a recurrent theme and subject to several major reviews after perceived shortcomings in a consistent policing approach. Protest and protesting is nothing new and is one of the ways in which a democratic society is sometimes defined, however, the Service is often left in a difficult and controversial position of balancing these rights with requirements to maintain law and order.

The future—Although difficult to predict the changes that the Service will undergo over the next few decades, it is clear that policing will always remain an important requirement for society. The most likely developments will probably be around the reduction in the number of forces and increased accountability by Chief Constables to deliver performance targets and meet financial efficiencies. But as we have seen from history, modern-day policing adapts in response to its surroundings and to socio-economic changes . . . who knows what the future will look like!

This chapter has been about giving you a brief look at how the Service has developed to reach its current status. After all, if you don't understand where you have come from it is very difficult to make sense of where you are. The Service has always been changing, yet remains focused on law enforcement and community reassurance. Nonetheless, if the almost unique character of British policing is to remain then the Service must maintain the support of the public. To this end amidst all the change, Peel's Nine Principles should remain the bedrock.

In the following chapters we will look at what drives the current Service at the strategic level and then how it organises itself to meet the present and future demands.

FURTHER READING

→ Clive Emsley, *The English Police: A Political and Social History*, 1996, Longman.
→ Clive Emsley, *Crime and Society in England, 1750–1900*, 2004, Longman.
→ Neil Walker, *Policing in a Changing Constitutional Order*, 2000, Sweet & Maxwell.

3

THE TRIPARTITE STRUCTURE

To the new or seasoned front-line police officer, who is usually busy dealing with responding to emergencies, investigating crime or arresting offenders, the wider political framework of how policing is directed and monitored is not something that apparently has any influence upon their duties.

However, it is because of the unique tripartite structure—the relationship between the Home Office, Police Authorities and Chief Constables—that is crucial in setting where policing priorities should be directed as well as what levels of performance are expected to be achieved.

This chapter will look at the roles of each of these parties in delivering policing services to the public.

Figure 3.1 The Tripartite Structure

3.1 **The Home Secretary**

Since 1853 the Home Secretary has been responsible for the overall stand-ard of policing in England and Wales and is accountable to Parliament. Despite being responsible, he or she does not have the power to direct how policing will be done.

Until relatively recently the Home Office relied entirely on an annual inspection of each force by Her Majesty's Inspectorate of Constabulary (HMIC) to ensure the efficiency of policing. HMIC is made up of a small number of former Chief Officers or senior public sector managers, together with their staff officers, who are seconded from different forces, and a small secretariat. Over the last few years, HMIC has evolved into an extremely influential and powerful body. Its working methods have changed dramatically over the past 20 years and HMIC can now be said to have two prime functions.

First, HMIC will look at how forces and police authorities across England and Wales are performing in relation to specific topics. These are known as 'Thematic Inspections', and the subsequently published reports are hugely influential and have become real drivers for change within the Service. Secondly, HMIC now looks at each force and authority in terms of the progress they are making with specific targets and recommenda-tions that have come from the centre and acting as a 'fierce advocate' of the public. Inspections of aspects of the work of specific forces may also be carried out at the direction of the Home Secretary.

For many years the Home Office attempted to exert influence, if not actual control, over how the individual forces worked by controlling who led them (Chief Constables can only be chosen from a list approved by the Home Office, and HMIC has a significant role in the appraisal of Chief Officers' performance). In addition the Home Office has for many years communicated its wishes directly to Chief Officers through what are known as 'Home Office Circulars'. These are in the shape of letters—signed, depending on their perceived importance, by very senior civil servants, Ministers of State or the Home Secretary, giving guidance as to what should be happening in each force. For example, it was Home Office circular 114/1983 that pushed forces to replacing officers in back office jobs, such as communications, with staff recruited specifically for those jobs. It had to be 'guidance' rather than instruction because the Home Secretary has no power to direct how forces will operate. That said, it is almost unknown for Home Office Circulars to be ignored.

Over recent years the Home Office has developed additional arms with which to ensure forces comply with its wishes. First, there is the National Policing Improvement Agency (NPIA). This is an agency of the Home Office that seeks to develop and promote best practice. This is a relatively new agency, but is becoming a very important one, with a key role in developing guidance and being responsible for national training and recruiting.

The Home Office sets and publishes its National Community Safety Plan. This lays down the strategic operational priorities that the Home Office wants to see forces and authorities concentrate on for a three-year period. The current National Plan is for the period 2008–11 and details requirements in such issues as reducing overall crime, increasing public confidence and increased partnership working.

3.2 **The Police Authorities**

Police authorities are made up of nine councillors from local authorities within the force area, and 'independent' members (one of whom must be a magistrate). The Metropolitan Police has a slightly different arrangement, in terms of the number and appointment of members including the Mayor of London (or his or her nominee), and its funding.

Police authorities are, then, independent of both local councils and central government. Outside London they raise a percentage of the money required to run their force, by means of a charge on the local council tax (known as the Police Precept). Their prime duty is to maintain an efficient and effective police service for their area and to hold the

Chief Officer to account; they also carry out other functions such as appointing the Chief Officer team, dealing with any complaints against them and also managing the Custody Visitor Scheme. As police forces are not a 'legal entity' it is the police authority that owns all property and is the employer of all police staff.

Local policing plans

The police authorities receive the National Policing Plan from the Home Office. They will then, through a system of ongoing local consultation with local authorities, community groups and public meetings, work with the Chief Constable to produce the Local Policing Plan (LPP). The LPP covers what their force will do for the following three years. It reflects, as it must, the national priorities and objectives set down by the Home Secretary and how those will be met. It will also include ways to tackle issues that are a priority for the local area.

The LPP will also set how the Service is paid for, the balance between central government grant and the money provided from council tax, and how the money is to be spent. For each area of service delivery that is set down the LPP will state not only what will be done, but how and— crucially—what the measure of success will be.

3.3 Chief Officers

The Chief Constables and Commissioners of the Metropolitan and City of London Police Forces are the third leg of the tripartite system of strategic police management. They are, as we have seen, appointed by the local police authority, albeit from a list of candidates approved by the Home Office, and are responsible for the delivery of policing for their force. They have operational command, which affords them considerable autonomy in how policing is carried out. They cannot, for example, be directed to pursue or not pursue a particular case. However, for their operational decisions they are accountable to the courts and the law, as is every officer under their command. For their management decisions they are accountable to their Police Authority. They, in practice, will need the authority's consent for major spending decisions and for how they structure their force. In particular, Chief Officers are responsible for meeting the priorities and targets set by the Police Authority and Home Office.

All Chief Officers are members of the Association of Chief Police Officers (ACPO), which is a professional body and has considerable influence over the Police Service. ACPO has an elected president, usually a Chief Constable, who will speak on behalf of the Service on policy issues, but has no authority over any police force. ACPO issues practice advice and guidance on a wide range of policing issues that forces are expected to adopt.

3.4 Performance Culture

Performance monitoring is not confined to the detection of crime but extends to every area of police work—how many intelligence reports officers submit (and their quality), how many stops and searches they make (and the results), how many and what incidents they attend (and the outcomes).

The drive to achieve results and demonstrate that best value for money is being attained now permeates the whole of the Service and the tools exist to ensure that everyone is playing their full part.

3.5 Accountability and Complaints

Another body that has progressively asserted its importance and influence is that of the Independent Police Complaints Commission (IPCC). This body was established under the Police Reform Act 2002 and became operational in 2004 in response to growing public concerns around confidence in the police complaints system.

The Commission is responsible for investigating serious complaints and allegations of misconduct against police officers. The IPCC has wide-ranging powers when it comes to investigations. It can choose the mode of investigation into matters, which can include managing or supervising local professional standards departments in their enquiries and evidence gathering or even conducting the investigation themselves.

The IPCC has worked hard to drive improvements and changes throughout the police service, consulting with police authorities and forces and making recommendations based on its investigation findings.

In Chapter 2 we saw how the police service developed and in this chapter we have looked at where the strategic imperatives that drive the Service come from, and how these arise. In the next chapter we look at how forces are organised to go about delivering the needs of our communities.

FURTHER READING

→ <http://www.hmic.gov.uk>. Website of Her Majesty's Inspectorate of Constabulary.
→ <http://www.acpo.co.uk>. Website of the Association of Chief Police Officers.
→ <http://www.homeoffice.gov.uk>. Website of the Home Office.
→ <http://www.ipcc.gov.uk>. Website of the Independent Police Complaints Commission.
→ <http://www.apa.police.uk>. Website of the Association of Police Authorities.

4

FORCE STRUCTURE AND ORGANISATION

In Chapter 2 we saw how the current 'policing landscape' came about and how we came to have the 43 territorial forces. Now it is time to look at how the forces are organised and how they go about their business. We will concentrate on the territorial forces—the so-called Home Office forces, but the role of the non-territorial forces is also explained.

4.1 The Forces

The 43 territorial forces cover the various counties and regions of England and Wales. Some forces police a single county and bear its name—West Yorkshire, Cumbria and Essex are good examples. Others cover a large city and the surrounding areas, or more than one county. Examples of these include West Midlands Police, Greater Manchester Police and Thames Valley Police. Figure 4.1 is a map showing the force boundaries.

Some forces carry the name 'Police', whilst others have 'Constabulary'. There is no significance to this; traditionally the old city and borough forces bore the title 'Police' whereas the County Forces were known as 'Constabularies'. However, over the years through amalgamations and re-branding exercises some forces, perhaps in an attempt to appear more modern, simply changed names (for example, Sussex Constabulary became Sussex Police in the early 1970s).

1. Avon & Somerset	16. Gwent	31. Nottinghamshire
2. Bedfordshire	17. Hampshire	32. South Wales
3. Cambridgeshire	18. Hertfordshire	33. South Yorkshire
4. Cheshire	19. Humberside	34. Staffordshire
5. City of London	20. Kent	35. Suffolk
6. Cleveland	21. Lancashire	36. Surrey
7. Cumbria	22. Leicestershire	37. Sussex
8. Derbyshire	23. Lincolnshire	38. Thames Valley
9. Devon & Cornwall	24. Merseyside	39. Warwickshire
10. Dorset	25. Metropolitan Police	40. West Mercia
11. Durham	26. Norfolk	41. West Midlands
12. Dyfed Powys	27. North Wales	42. West Yorkshire
13. Essex	28. North Yorkshire	43. Wiltshire
14. Gloucestershire	29. Northamptonshire	
15. Greater Manchester	30. Northumbria	

Figure 4.1 The Territorial Police Forces in England and Wales

Source: The Home Office

© Crown copyright material is reproduced with the permission of the Controller of HMSO and Queen's Printer for Scotland.

Non-territorial forces

When we have looked at how the Service has developed we have considered only those police forces that are based on geographical areas, the counties and cities of England and Wales. There are other forces which do an important job and deserve a brief mention here.

British Transport Police

The British Transport Police, affectionately known by its initials, BTP, has its origins in the early days of the railways. It now numbers around 2,300 officers and is responsible for policing the railways across the whole of the UK, including the London Underground and the Docklands Light Railway. BTP officers are recruited using the same process as in territorial forces and receive the same basic training to which they add their own specialist courses.

Ministry of Defence Police

The Ministry of Defence Police performs the same sort of investigative role as territorial forces in relation to crimes committed on the Ministry's property. However, its prime focus is providing armed security at defence sites throughout the UK. Every member of this force is trained in the use of firearms, but it also has the largest fraud investigation department of any force in the UK.

Civil Nuclear Constabulary

Formerly the UK Atomic Energy Authority Constabulary, this force was reconstituted on 1 April 2005 under an independent police authority. It has just over 600 officers and is responsible for guarding some designated licensed civil nuclear energy sites in the UK and ensuring the safe transit of designated nuclear material. Like the Ministry of Defence Police, all its members are trained in the use of firearms, and most are armed each day.

4.2 **Internal Structure**

As we saw in Chapter 2, forces originally followed the organisational model of the Metropolitan Police. There was a force headquarters, which included central service functions, and a number of territorial divisions commanded by a Superintendent that policed a geographical area. Over the years the rank structure expanded and divisional commanders became Chief Superintendents. Divisions in most forces were subdivided into operational commands, known as sub-divisions, each run by a Superintendent, with a Chief Inspector as second-in-command. This organisational model lasted until the early 1990s.

In 1990 the Audit Commission, a government body set up to ensure best value for public money is achieved, suggested that the command pyramid needed to be flatter, following the management trend of the time. It recommended removing the divisional layer so that there was just a Force Headquarters and territorial operational units answerable directly to the force commanders. Such operational commands were to be known as Basic Command Units (BCUs). Over the next few years most, if not all, forces adopted this model, though not all took on the nomenclature and continued to use the term Division.

More recently, following the introduction of Crime and Disorder Reduction Partnerships, another model is being adopted nationwide— that of Neighbourhood Policing. We will look in detail at how this works at street level in Chapter 6, so for now we only need to look at the top level effects.

The Force Headquarters consists of the command element made up of Chief Officers (see the description of the rank structure at section 4.3 below), administration, training and finance, and those specialist units which have a force-wide responsibility.

In each force the BCUs will usually have their boundaries aligned to those of local authorities; each will be commanded, depending on the force, by a Superintendent or Chief Superintendent. A BCU can be thought of as a miniature police force. It will have its own headquarters with administrative and finance staff and specialist units such as CID and intelligence officers.

The number of BCUs and their units will vary from force to force, however, a typical structure will be similar to that shown in Figure 4.2.

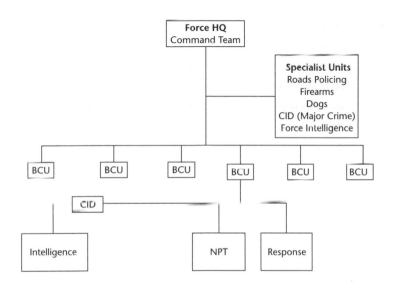

Figure 4.2 Typical force organisational structure

4.3 **The Rank Structure**

Whilst most officers spend most of their time working alone, policing is a team game. Each person has their role and together the effect is greater than the sum of parts. Additionally, you will attend many incidents that need the efforts of several officers to deal with them successfully and safely. Note the 'safely'; policing can be a dangerous business and as a police officer your prime duty is the safety of the public and then, and only then, the safety of your colleagues and finally yourself.

Most of the time you will be responsible for making your own decisions as to what should be done; however, when a team effort is needed then someone has to be in charge and they need to be able to give orders that will be obeyed. Very often on these occasions someone will get hurt, or even killed, if what needs to be done is not done promptly and efficiently.

It is for this reason that the police have preserved a formal rank structure (as indeed have other linked organisations such as the Fire and Rescue Service). When the modern police service was founded in 1829, society was based on a recognised hierarchy, and the pseudo-military ranks used in the police were a natural extension of it. Today we may be used to far more egalitarian ways, but when it is a matter of life and death there can be no room for discussion and argument. So the rank structure is maintained.

Figure 4.3 shows the badges of rank in 41 of the 43 Home Office forces. The Metropolitan and City of London police forces have a slightly different structure above Chief Superintendent.

All police officers join via the same process and though some may be promoted (there is the High Potential Development Scheme for those identified as having the potential to reach the highest ranks), all hold the office of constable, as we noted in Chapter 1.

The first step is to be confirmed as a constable. Whilst it is true that for the first two years you will undergo your basic training (we will look at what this entails later in the book), you will at the same time be a student officer in what is still referred to as the 'probation' phase. The word 'probation' comes from the Latin word *probare*—to put to the test, and that is what 'The Job' will be doing to you. As well as passing your training you have to prove—to your force, to your colleagues and, most importantly, to yourself—that you are good enough to be a police officer.

Constable   Sergeant   Inspector   Chief Inspector

Superintendent   Chief   Assistant Chief
             Superintendent   Constable
                        (Commander in
                        Metropolitan)

Deputy Chief   Chief Constable   Deputy   Commissioner
Constable   (Assistant   Commissioner (Metropolitan only)
(Deputy Assistant Commissioner (Metropolitan only)
Commissioner in Metropolitan)
in Metropolitan)

Figure 4.3 Badges of rank

Source: The Metropolitan Police

Once confirmed if you want to go for promotion you will first of all need to pass the national qualifying examination for sergeant. This is a multiple-choice paper on law and procedure, and requires an in-depth knowledge of both if you are going to pass it. The exam does not, in itself, get you promoted however; it is merely the joining ticket. Once you have passed the written paper then, depending on your force, you will either have to pass a nationally run assessment centre or an interview board followed by a 12-month period of workplace assessment whilst performing the role of sergeant on a temporary basis. The workplace assessment is a recent innovation and, at the time of writing, has not yet been adopted nationally. Where it is not yet available, officers seeking to qualify for promotion will have to pass the nationally run assessment centre, which is strictly speaking the second part of the qualifying examination.

As a sergeant you will either be in charge of a team of constables and Police Community Support Officers (PCSOs) policing a small area, or around eight constables on a support team. Your job will primarily be to ensure that your people do what is needed and do it efficiently and effectively. In addition you will be the person in command of larger incidents requiring the effort of a small team.

The next rank is that of Inspector. Again you will need to pass the national qualifying examination (a multiple-choice examination on the relevant law) and then, as with the constable to sergeant procedure, either an assessment centre or a period of workplace assessment in the role. As an Inspector you will be responsible for taking the policy directions handed down from above and turning them into actions that your sergeants can get their teams to deliver, often in liaison with other agencies. You will also be expected to take operational command of critical incidents that need a significant number of people to manage.

Promotion above Inspector is based on performance in your current rank and sometimes an assessment centre. There are no more formal examinations. At the level of Chief Inspector and above, whilst you will be expected to take charge of serious incidents and large-scale events, your primary role will be one of strategy and longer term planning rather than day-to-day police work.

One thing that needs to be mentioned here is the issue of modes of address. As was noted earlier, there are times when a person in charge has to be able to give an order and know that it will be obeyed. Experience has shown that this level of action requires a certain formality in the relationship between those at different levels. Therefore, whilst on duty, sergeants are addressed as 'Sergeant' and Inspectors and above are addressed as 'Sir' or 'Ma'am' as appropriate. In specialist departments and later on in your service these rules may be relaxed somewhat, but, for the early part of your service at least, you will have to get used to them.

4.4 **Crime Boundaries and the National Intelligence Model**

All crime has to happen in someone's 'local' policing area, but the overwhelming majority of crime is 'local' in that its effects are limited to people living or working within a small geographical area. A great deal of recorded crime involves acts of vandalism and 'low-level' violence. Secondly, even so-called acquisitive crime (theft and similar offences) is generally committed by people and against people who both live and work in a relatively confined area; there was a study done some years ago which showed that most burglars 'worked' within a mile of their home address. Therefore, it makes sense for the majority of police effort to be based on prevention, detection and finding solutions to underlying causes within local communities.

However, what might appear to be local crime quite often has links to a wider group of criminals. If policing is going to have any effect it must be organised to work at all levels and this is where the National Intelligence Model and the current round of police reform comes in.

For many years solving each individual crime in their case-load was the aim of each officer; and, don't be mistaken, getting detections is still a primary aim as we saw when we looked at the performance culture in Chapter 3 and as we will see again when we look at real world policing in Part II. However, some years ago it was finally realised that treating each case as single and distinct was, for the most part, inefficient. Some crimes are indeed one-offs, most murders would fall into this category, but probably the majority are part of a pattern of behaviour by one or more individuals. The principle of intelligence-led policing, where the totality of crime is considered and police actions are targeted accordingly, came to the fore in the early 1990s. Since then it has gradually been developed and refined into the National Intelligence Model (NIM).

The NIM recognises the need to impact at three levels.

- **Level 1**—Local issues. Usually crimes, criminals and other problems that affect at a local level, no wider than a BCU. Whilst such issues may vary from low value thefts and vandalism to very serious crimes such as murder, in themselves the crimes do not need a wider view, though they may provide information which can be turned into intelligence which, when developed, may affect a higher tier.
- **Level 2**—Cross border issues. Here we are talking about criminal behaviour by an individual or groups that affect more than one BCU or, more importantly, more than one force area.
- **Level 3**—Serious organised crime on a national or international scale, which requires identification by proactive means and a response by teams dedicated to working at this level.

To make the understanding of these levels easier a real life example may help.

EXAMPLE

Tommy is a heroin addict. To satisfy his addiction he needs considerable sums of money which he raises by burgling houses and business premises near where he lives, interspersed with a bit of shoplifting. Tommy buys his drugs from a dealer in the town centre who, in turn, gets them from a 'wholesaler' in the nearest big city. The wholesaler gets them from the importer elsewhere in the country who is part of a gang which has connections through to the Middle East.

Tommy's crimes are part of a chain which has links at many levels: at neighbourhood level (where he steals); at the BCU level (where his dealer sells)—level 1; at the regional or force level (the activities of the wholesaler)—level 2; and at national and international level (the importer)—level 3.

With these levels in mind, look again at the force structure diagram (Figure 4.2). You can see that at the BCU level there is an intelligence unit. All officers within the BCU will be contributing the information they collect during their work to this unit. There the information is analysed and fed back to inform the work of the BCU teams and where relevant it is fed up the chain to the Force Intelligence Unit, which is under the command of force HQ. Here they will be looking for and at issues which affect more than one BCU. They will also be exchanging information with the Serious Organised Crime Agency (SOCA), which is charged with dealing with the national response to level 3 criminality.

You may have thought that forces can look after crimes and criminals who work across BCUs and that SOCA deals with national and international matters, but what happens with crime issues which affect more than one force but do not meet the criteria for level 3?

This gap at level 2 is now increasingly filled by joint squads and units that are formed between forces or established on a regional basis involving several forces.

Policing is, as you will have gathered by now, a fast changing occupation. Of all the initiatives and reforms that have been introduced over the last few years the advent of the NIM is probably one of the most far-reaching and profound in terms of its effect on the work of front-line officers, yet it is one of the least remarked upon. As and when you join the Service it will repay your effort many times over for you to take the time to gain an in-depth understanding of its processes and products.

In this chapter we have looked at how the Home Office forces are organised, the rank structure and the prime method now being used to manage their business (note that these last two apply equally to non-Home Office forces). When taken in conjunction with the previous chapters you will now have an idea about the complexity of modern policing, but apart from a look at the office of constable we have said very little about the people involved. It is now time to rectify that omission and in the next chapter we will look at some of the roles that have to be performed if the Service is going to function.

FURTHER READING

→ <http://www.homeoffice.gov.uk>—website of the Home Office.
→ <http://www.mod.police.uk>—website of the Ministry Of Defence Police.
→ <http://www.btp.police.uk>—website of the British Transport Police.
→ <http://www.cnc.police.uk>—website of the Civil Nuclear Constabulary.
→ <http://www.soca.gov.uk>—website of the Serious and Organised Crime Agency.

5

THE POLICE FAMILY

Although the business of modern day policing has become increasingly complex, with a multitude of pressures on the Police Service, the actual job of working as an officer remains as exciting and challenging as ever. With a wide breadth of career paths and opportunities to choose from, today's modern officer can benefit from high standards of training and support, which is almost unparalleled within any other employment sector.

This chapter looks at some of the main roles that officers and staff occupy within the Service and explains what they do and the type of policing areas they cover. The list is not exhaustive, but gives a flavour of the many areas of work that are available.

5.1 Police Officers

Every police officer holds the office of constable and is individually sworn into the role by a local magistrate. There are around 140,000 regular officers in England and Wales, who all start as student officers and receive the same initial national training.

Officers typically spend the first two years of their service in uniform roles. This time is spent gradually building their experience through the aid of a tutor constable on either a Response Team, answering 999 calls and processing offenders, or with a Neighbourhood Policing Team, where the new officer is expected to develop a knowledge and understanding of the management of community based quality of life issues, such as reducing anti-social behaviour.

After successful completion of this initial phase, officers can then look towards applying for different roles or consider applying for promotion. However, many officers choose to remain at the rank of constable and are happy to continue their service without entering into any specialist areas. Short attachments usually assist officers in making the right career choices.

Response team

Whatever the incident, whether day or night, officers on response teams represent the backbone of the police service in dealing with crime and public safety emergencies. Whether on mobile or foot patrol, response team officers work in uniform and are led by an Inspector or Sergeant. They are responsible for responding to a wide variety of calls as well as giving support to other specialist units.

From domestic disputes or a suspicious death, a burglary, street robbery or shoplifter, pub fight or major disaster, it is usually a response team officer who is first at the scene. These officers need to be able to use good judgement in diffusing potentially dangerous or violent situations as well as being calm under pressure when coordinating the initial response to larger incidents.

For many, the situations and associated skills attached to front-line police work provide common reasons for joining the service. These officers play a crucial role in maintaining public confidence in law enforcement as well as being seen to be fair, professional and competent in their duties.

A large majority of officers choose to remain in this busy and exciting front-line role and take pride in overcoming the challenges of policing at the sharp-end.

Neighbourhood Policing Teams (NPTs)

Based in the heart of communities and focusing upon longer-term problem solving, NPTs have a key role in building confidence in the police. After directives from central government, these teams were established to give easily recognised and visible links with the community. NPTs support local areas through the management of Partners and Community Together (PACT) meetings. These meetings provide communities with a forum to raise local problems, define police priorities and access other services.

Teams are often mixed, comprising of both officers and PCSOs, and work closely with other local agencies, such as the council, schools and voluntary sectors. This ensures they are able to mobilise combined action in tackling a wide variety of crime and anti-social issues.

Unlike the role of the traditional local 'community constable', NPTs focus more dynamically in solving problems and can often be seen reassuring and explaining police actions and initiatives within communities. This is busy work, especially in more complex community environments, and requires officers to have an intimate understanding of their locality as well as an ability to use imaginative approaches in resolving issues.

Criminal Investigation Department (CID)

Often the basis for fictional film and television characters, working as a detective within the CID is often the career choice for those wishing to specialise in the investigation of crime and more serious incidents. Although criminal investigation is not just the preserve of the CID, when it comes to more complex, time-consuming and high profile cases, then CID detectives are likely to take the lead.

Detectives need to be able to combine excellent inquiry and interviewing skills, matched with a heightened knowledge of areas such as criminal legislation and legal processes, forensics, case file preparation, as well as working with the Crown Prosecution Service.

Criminal Investigation Departments have changed significantly over the past decade, focusing more closely on proactive work, rather than just reacting to crimes. This has changed the profile of units with little left of the 'us and them' attitude to uniform colleagues that used to exist. There still remains considerable competition for places within CID, as many officers may spend their careers as a detective, or use these skills to progress further into other specialist work, such as major crime, fraud investigation, robbery squads or Counter-Terrorism Units.

All detectives attend a crime investigation course, with continuous assessment in the workplace through the Professionalising Investigation Process (PIP), which ensures they maintain their skills as criminal investigators.

Roads policing

Highly skilled in traffic law and collision investigation, with responsibility for policing major roads and motorways, roads policing officers are experts in their field. Most forces have seen the overall capacity of roads policing officers fall over the past few years, but this has been matched by a dramatic rise in their capabilities.

Roads policing has undergone a state of the art transformation, with high performance vehicles and highly trained officers benefitting from the introduction of new technologies, such as Automatic Number Plate Recognition (ANPR) systems. This new technology allows officers to be alerted to stolen or suspicious vehicles connected to crime activities by a computerised system in their patrol car.

These improvements have also meant a change to the approach of roads policing units, which have shed the traditional image of the 'Traffic Officer', instead focusing upon their crime fighting abilities in addition to making road travel as safe as it can be.

Roads policing officers, who are identified by a white cap, have a valuable role to play in targeting criminals on the roads network, by gathering intelligence about their movements and intercepting them when least expected.

Firearms support

In response to the most serious and dangerous criminals and those who arm themselves with firearms, the police service has developed specialist units to deal with this threat. These units are made up of Authorised Firearms Officers (AFOs), who are recognised and selected on the basis of their operational abilities.

All AFOs are volunteers and are deployed to high-risk situations involving guns and lethal weapons. Such situations often involve unpredictable and dangerous armed suspects and armed officers need to be highly trained and tested to nationally set standards. Officers are subject to frequent re-qualification in areas of tactics, physical fitness, weapons handling and accuracy skills.

In addition, AFOs are also expected to be skilled in advanced driving and specialist vehicle tactics. As armed incidents are not common, these officers spend a lot of their time on patrol in support of uniformed colleagues until required. With further specialist skills available in areas such as VIP close-protection, hostage rescue and rifle expertise, this career route has tremendous opportunities for any officer who wishes to test their skills in the most dangerous of policing situations.

Specialist crime

Although local CID officers are involved in day-to-day crime detection and investigations, specialist units focus upon a variety of policing work, including targeting organised crime groups and drug suppliers. The nature of this sort of work means that these units are often covert in their activities and may work from purpose-built facilities. Criminal cases that go before the courts may be down to years of painstaking work by specialist crime units, who utilise state-of-the-art methods of evidence gathering and surveillance.

Taking on this role means that detectives and support staff need to be highly dedicated to their work in bringing serious criminals to justice.

Child and public protection

Another career route for investigators is in the area of child and public protection, an aspect of policing that has expanded greatly over the years. This is in part down to several high-profile cases, which revealed weaknesses in protecting some of the most vulnerable people in society. Working closely with social services, health professionals and charity groups, protection work requires highly resilient officers who can conduct investigations when faced with harrowing situations, often involving traumatised victims.

Tactical support

Although many uniformed officers are trained in basic public order, tactical support officers are trained to the highest national standards in public order and public safety techniques. The term 'Riot Police', often used by media sources when serious disorder breaks out, belies the many skills tactical support officers have, including specialist search skills and dealing with violent or disturbed people.

Officers work in close-knit teams who train and work together and usually cover entire force areas in support of uniform and plain-clothes colleagues. Tactical support officers are on hand to make difficult entries to fortified drug dealing premises, or are called in when local units are struggling to control violent groups on a busy night in a city or town centre.

Linked to these units are waterborne specialists, who are trained in underwater search techniques, which are used in rescue and evidence recovery.

Mounted and dog sections

The modern police family includes not only officers and support staff, but also a host of trained animals who have a valuable contribution to make to law enforcement and community safety. Both mounted and dog support sections have a long association with policing that stretches back to the formation of the modern-day Police Service. Mounted officers are used for general patrol, at community events, as well as at large-scale public order incidents. Police horses are highly trained and tested to ensure they stay under control in public environments.

Police dogs, both general purpose and specialist drug or explosive detection, are often viewed as an essential part of any police team. Competition to be a dog handler is always tough, but requires officers to take care of their dogs both at work and off-duty. Regular training is a key part of this role, so is the expectation of being fit and being able to follow their dog through all sorts of terrain. This career choice really is a rewarding, but full-time commitment.

Air support

Police career choices do not always have to remain on the ground! Since the development of air support units around the country, officers can train to be air observers and take on this unique role. Police helicopters are a regular sight, particularly in urban forces, but their role is often not fully understood by the public, who can often view them as a noisy and expensive nuisance. However, with a host of technological instruments capable of assisting ground officers in crime fighting, search and vehicle pursuit operations, air support units have proved their worth as a valuable platform from which to protect the public from the skies.

Counter-Terrorism Units (CTU) and Special Branch

Since the tragic attacks of September 2001 in New York and of July 2005 in London, the Police Service has dramatically altered its approach and structures in meeting the new challenges faced by the threat of terrorist groups. Although the threat posed by Irish related groups has diminished over recent years, due in the main to political changes, challenges related to terrorism from Al-Qaeda and extreme right-wing groups has meant this is a busy area of policing.

In response, CTUs were recently established across the country to tackle domestic and violent extremism from whichever source it may come from. Acting not just as an enforcement body, CTUs gather intelligence and engage with communities to help prevent and deter terrorism.

Ensuring the safety of airports and ports, special branch officers work closely with Borders and Immigration officers and can exercise additional powers to protect the country's borders. Like CTUs, special branch officers also have a role in liaising with the Security Services (MI5) and investigating any threat to national security.

Additional skills

The above roles are just some of the main specialist areas where officers can progress their careers, however, this list is not exhaustive and this whole book could be dedicated to all the roles that the police service has to offer! However, if a full-time specialist role is not for you, officers can gain additional skills that provide extra variety to general policing duties.

Some of the main additional skill areas are in public order, student officer tutoring, training, specialist interviewing and victim care, as well as Chemical, Biological, Radiological Nuclear (CBRN) training and response.

One thing you are guaranteed by choosing a police career is variety. There is no excuse for getting bored or tied down to one policing area and this is one reason why so many officers have such fulfilling careers.

5.2 Police Support Staff

Police officers are a highly trained and expensive resource who have extensive skills and are adaptable to a wide-range of policing environments. Police support staff colleagues, who have progressively released officers back to the front-line or core policing roles over the last few years, complement these skills.

'Civilianisation' and 'Workforce Modernisation' are policing terms that describe this process, which has greatly benefitted the service by effectively using specifically trained staff to carry out essential and important roles.

Some of these roles include:

- Communication officers
- Public enquiry desk clerks
- Crime analysts
- Administration and computer support personnel
- Detention officers
- Project, finance and training staff
- Police community support officers (PCSOs)
- Scenes of crime officers (SOCOs).

These are all careers that have expanded dramatically as the police service continues to look at modern and efficient ways of working.

This structural change has not always been easy for the Police Service to adopt. But the expansion of police support staff into roles that were once the preserve of police officers has meant that specialist non-policing skills can be used more effectively to deliver a first-class service to the public. As you can see, policing is a complex business, more than just front-line law enforcement.

5.3 Special Constables

With the same uniform, same powers and same equipment as a regular constable, members of the special constabulary, or 'specials' as they are commonly referred to, are an addition to policing operations, and in turn, to improved community reassurance.

Facing the same risks as a regular officer, this is a crime-fighting role with a difference—the really special part being that officers are fully sworn, but perform this role on a voluntary basis, giving up their time for no financial reward.

Specials are usually deployed at times of additional demand, such as at weekends or for local events. This means regular officers can benefit from extra resources or be released to focus on other crime-fighting activities.

With comprehensive training in law and procedures, being a law enforcement volunteer can be difficult to fit on top of another job. Specials offer a great deal to their communities and the police family, with many going on to become regular officers. Forces are always seeking additional volunteers to take on this role and anyone who is seeking a career in the police service can get an insight into the work through being a special constable and decide if policing is right for them.

This chapter has looked at the astounding range of roles that make up the wider police family. Whatever the role, whether in uniform or plain clothes, sworn officer or support staff, the policing family is all about teamwork and combining these skills into an effective force in the service of the community.

In the next part of the book we look at the job of a police officer and what it is like to actually do it.

PART II

THE JOB

6

A POLICE OFFICER'S JOB

In this chapter we take a look at what policing is about, what has to be done.

As we saw in Chapter 2, modern policing in England and Wales dates back to the founding of the Metropolitan Police on 29 September 1829. Richard Mayne, one of the joint Commissioners, laid down the ethos of the new service when he wrote:

> The primary object of an efficient police is the prevention of crime: the next that of detection and punishment of offenders if crime is committed. To these ends all the efforts of police must be directed. The protection of life and property, the preservation of public tranquillity, and the absence of crime, will alone prove whether those efforts have been successful and whether the objects for which the police were appointed have been attained.

Essentially the role of the police in England and Wales has not changed in over 170 years, since the 'New Police' was founded. However, in that time society has changed dramatically, and become far more complex and sophisticated in the process. Additionally, because policing is rooted in the society it serves, policing has likewise become far more complex and sophisticated. So let's look at what the modern Service needs to do in pursuit of the 'Primary Object' and how it goes about its work.

6.1 Maintaining a Tranquil Society

There are three tasks under this heading: keeping the peace, preventing crime and, just as importantly, reducing the fear of crime. Originally, and until quite recently, the primary method used to do all three was to have constables patrolling a defined area on foot and dealing with whatever they came across as they walked their beat. Being on foot, the officers were approachable, and had the time to see what was happening around them and deal with it. There is no doubt that this method of policing was popular with the public, as shown by the frequent calls for more 'Bobbies on the beat' still to be heard almost daily from the press, community leaders and politicians. Unfortunately, the 'Bobbie on the Beat' model of policing requires a large number of officers if it is to be effective.

From the early 1960s the growth in both population and town size was not matched by a corresponding increase in police numbers. Additionally the amount of crime reported by the public rocketed during the same period (in London there were a total of 188,000 crimes reported in 1960, for 2003 the figure was 1,058,000). As well as reporting more crimes, the public demands on the Service have dramatically increased, and people have become increasingly more sophisticated in how they want their demands to be met. To satisfy these requirements, more and more officers have had to be taken from beat duty and into specialist posts, leaving insufficient numbers to provide an effective service using the traditional model.

The first thing to note is that preventing crime and keeping the peace is no longer something the Police Service is expected to tackle on its own. As a result of the Crime and Disorder Act 1998 every local area has a Crime and Disorder Reduction Partnership (CDRP). CDRPs bring together the police, police authorities, local authorities, other agencies and businesses in the area to develop and implement strategies for stopping and if necessary dealing with crime and disorderly behaviour.

The latest policing model, which has been adopted throughout England and Wales, involves force internal boundaries to be aligned to those of the local authority, thus creating a clear link between the policing team for an area and the CDRP. Furthermore, within those internal boundaries, beats will be aligned to one or more council wards and each beat will have a dedicated Neighbourhood Policing Team (NPT).

These teams look at crime and disorder locally and make an assessment to see whether the offending and/or anti-social behaviour is part of a pattern that degrades the quality of life for all concerned—victims, neighbours and offenders. If it is part of a pattern the NPT will work with other agencies (for example, housing, street lighting—whatever is needed) to come up with a solution that will at least break the pattern. The key point here is that any policing response is now directed to some clear purpose as part of an overall plan.

An obvious example is targeted patrolling related to keeping the peace in city or town centres at night. It is regrettably a sad fact of life that on Thursday, Friday and Saturday nights substantial numbers of people will visit the pubs and clubs and get drunk. The consequent and all too frequent public disorder requires numerous police officers to be deployed.

Another cause for officers in uniform to be deployed in substantial numbers is events such as large-scale public demonstrations, football matches, carnivals or outdoor pop concerts. All such events require a great deal of pre-planning by the police who work with event organisers to ensure that public safety and public order is maintained. However, problems can occur and trouble makers may need to be arrested or contained as quickly as possible. The role of officers deployed to such events will vary from being deployed to patrol at certain locations, monitor crowds or to being part of a specially equipped and trained Police Support Unit (PSU) to be deployed in the event of serious trouble.

6.2 Investigation of Crime

Once a crime has been committed it is the job of the police to gather the evidence and put the facts (and evidence) before the Crown Prosecution Service (CPS). It is no longer the role of the police to put the offender before the court and it certainly is not their task to become involved in the punishment of offenders.

Of course it will be your job to identify the offender and, where necessary and appropriate, to arrest them, but the arrest should nowadays be thought of as part of the evidence-gathering process. The CPS will, except in the most trivial of cases, be involved in advising what additional evidence needs to be obtained and when the accused should be charged and with what offence. The decision to charge is now not a decision that you or any other police officer can take.

Crime can be thought of as falling into four categories:

- major crime (for example, murder);
- specialist crime (for example, sophisticated frauds);
- priority crime (for example, burglary of people's homes); and
- volume crime (for example, minor theft, taking cars without consent).

Major crimes are investigated by teams of detectives headed by a senior officer who has been trained and is qualified for the role of Senior Investigating Officer (SIO). Such crimes involving children or which otherwise generate a high profile and huge public interest can require teams several dozen strong.

Detectives are specialists in the investigation of crime, but some crimes are so complex by their nature that they require specialist detectives to investigate them; economic crime falls into this category.

Priority crimes are crimes which may be quite common, yet are sufficiently disturbing to the public that the force has decided to detect as many as possible by ensuring that they are investigated by detectives. The burglary of someone's home would be a typical example. The list of crimes in this category may differ from force to force, as will the procedures to be followed before the CID take over, but as a uniformed officer you will commonly be the first officer to attend the scene and you will be expected to start the investigation off.

Volume crimes are the most common offences and are the ones that are generally regarded as less serious—though remember the victims may have a different view. Response and Neighbourhood Policing Team officers will be expected to carry out the whole investigation from the initial report through, hopefully, to detection and final disposal. Sometimes it is clear from the outset who the offender is, and all the evidence, including the arrest of the offender, can be gathered very quickly. Sometimes it is equally obvious very quickly that there is almost no hope of ever gathering sufficient evidence to identify let alone prosecute the offender.

As part of any investigation, officers are required to interview witnesses and take statements. This can sometimes be a difficult and traumatic experience for witnesses, especially if the crime has been violent or sexually motivated and officers need to be sympathetic and sensitive as well as gaining evidence, which may lead to a conviction a court.

6.3 **General Police Duties**

Over the years, the Police Service has taken on more and more responsibilities. In part the Service was given, or took on, these responsibilities simply because it is always there. Twenty-four hours a day every day of the year the police are available to the public; almost from the beginning, they have been the agency of last resort for anyone with a problem. Remember too that many of the public agencies that now seem obvious candidates for some police roles simply did not exist until relatively recently. The other reason why the extra responsibilities came to the Service was that if the matters were not dealt with properly then crime and/or disorder was likely to follow, so it was in the best interest of society that the police took them on.

These sundry roles and responsibilities are known as general police duties, let's look at some of them.

Patrol

Taking to the streets for the first time in uniform, whether it be on foot or in a patrol car, is a moment that will last with you throughout your career: a combination of pride and sheer terror for some officers! But this is what the public perceive as a core duty of police officers, being present to reassure the public and maintain law and order. Patrol is exciting and officers have many skills to learn, not just the theory of legal powers, but how to deal with incidents, what to do, how to make effective and quick decisions and when to call for additional help. The basic skills of policing learnt at this stage will likely influence the rest of your career as patrolling gives a wide breadth of experience in most aspects of police work.

Sudden death

When a person dies the death must be reported to the coroner for the area unless a medical practitioner can immediately certify the cause of death and that it was from natural causes; there are strict rules governing when such a certificate can be issued. Although coroners have their own officers to make follow-up enquiries and deal with the administration, unless the death happened in a hospital or hospice or such similar place, a police officer will have to attend the scene. Your job will be to examine the body and the scene to ensure that there are no indications that the death involved a criminal offence (if there is any such suggestion, then, of course, you will be treating it as a crime scene and the wheels for a homicide investigation will start to turn) and to speak to any relatives or witnesses to gather the initial evidence on which the coroner can base the decisions in the case.

Licensing

The sale and consumption of alcohol have, as we have seen, a strong and direct link with disorder on the streets. Since the Licensing Act 1872 the police have always had an involvement in enforcing the regulations and restrictions applied to licensed premises. Since the most recent Act came into force in 2005, the Service now takes a far more partnership-based approach with local authorities. Nevertheless, you can expect to be involved with ensuring pubs and clubs are being run correctly and lawfully.

Missing persons

When a person, be it a child or an adult, goes missing it is to the police that people naturally turn, and over the years it has become established that the police have a common law duty to investigate such reports. After a number of high profile cases, there is now a national protocol as to how missing person cases are to be investigated. Whilst it is not appropriate to go into detail here, the key element is that all reports are treated from the basis that the disappearance is crime-related until the contrary can be shown. Particular attention will always be paid to missing children and vulnerable adults, as they are at the most risk of being the victim of criminals. Though the national protocol suggests that an Inspector is always the officer in charge of a missing person enquiry, it is usually the job of a constable to take the initial report and conduct enquiries.

Mental health

People with mental health difficulties tend to be amongst the most vulnerable in society. Some with particular conditions will often come to the notice of the police because of their behaviour in public. Only in a very small minority of cases will they present a danger to others; they are far more likely to be at risk themselves. As a uniformed officer you can expect to be the first officer to respond to such cases and you will have powers under the Mental Health Act 1983 to remove the person to a place of safety if it is necessary to do so for their own protection.

Roads policing

You will also be expected to attend and assist at road traffic collisions (RTCs). The police do not call them accidents, because most of them are not accidents. Those involving death or serious injury will be dealt with by specialist traffic officers.

As a uniformed officer, you will also want to bear in mind that very few crimes do not involve the use of a motor vehicle. Even if the car is not directly used in the crime, criminals may use one to go about their business and whilst they are driving they may be committing other traffic-related offences.

6.4 Intelligence

Although moves were made in the early to mid-1990s to move towards 'intelligence-led policing', it has only been with the formulation and adoption of the National Intelligence Model (NIM) that a coherent and useful method of working at all levels—local, force-wide and national/international—of the Service has been possible.

Some parts of the police intelligence arena are the preserve of specialists. For example, the handling of informants, which now comes under the title of Covert Human Intelligence Sources (CHIS), can only be undertaken by officers with particular training. However, intelligence is symmetrical; the quality of the output depends on the quality of the inputs. If the information going into the system is lacking then nothing useful is ever going to come out of it.

In this chapter we have looked at some of the key elements that go into modern policing. There are of course more that could have been mentioned, national security work and the tactical use of firearms to name but two. But as these are far outside the experience of most officers in their early years of service they really fall outside the scope of this book. During your training and certainly once you have achieved independent patrol status you will be expected to deal with all the tasks mentioned above. But just dealing with the incidents is only one part of the job of policing; how they are dealt with, ensuring that the needs of victims, witnesses and all those that call for the services of the police are met and respected are themes that are covered in race and diversity training. Such training aims to impress upon officers the need to understand differences within society and that simple steps in the treatment of people can have immense effects upon the way that the police are trusted and approached, particularly by vulnerable groups within the community. Diversity training may include understanding race, sexuality, gender, faith and disability and are important issues that are constantly revisited as part of officer development. The next few chapters look at the roles and the qualities required of police officers in further detail.

7

REALITY CHECK

Research carried out by a university into the motivations of recruits in a county force showed that most of them had got their impressions of what policing was like from television programmes. The reality, as you may well by now have realised, is somewhat far from that projected in programmes like 'The Bill' and 'The Sweeney'. Experienced trainers have noted some facts of life about policing seem to come as a shock to some recruits and, too often, are the cause of their resignations. So in this chapter we will explore some of those issues.

> '*I wanted a profession that was varied, challenging, and different and in the public service – policing has fulfilled all of those and more.*'
> **Chief Constable of a county force**

> '*I wanted to be dealing with people, and I felt I wanted to make a difference to others.*'
> **PC in a county force**

7.1 **Shift Work**

Most people realise that policing is a service that is provided for 24 hours every day of the year. Strange as it may seem, not every recruit realises that this may mean having to work through the night, regardless of one's gender and age. Different forces have different shift patterns, so it is not possible to say here how the work rota is organised for the force you may be interested in joining. What you can be sure of is that there are days when you will be starting early in the morning (06:00 or 07:00 are common), days when you will be starting in the afternoon (any time between 14:00 and 18:00) and working through the evening, and days when you may work a night shift (usually starting at 21:00 or 22:00).

You will notice that no finishing times were given; this was deliberate. Nowadays shifts are usually planned to be between eight and ten hours long. However, what is planned and what actually happens are all too frequently different things. If you have arrested someone or are otherwise involved in a job, you will generally be required to stay on duty until you have either finished all that needs to be done for the time being or you have got to the point that the job can be handed on to someone else *and* there is someone else to hand it on to.

You will not have a choice in this and it means that you will frequently be late getting home, sometimes by many hours. Current legislation ensures that officers have a minimum amount of time off between shifts, but this still means that you will frequently get tired.

There is also the added necessity of sometimes working on your allotted days off. This is usually because of large operations requiring considerable numbers of officers. There is no choice in this as a police officer is obliged to work when required and if your force needs you to work on your days off then, unless you resign, you have no choice but to do so. It should be said that all hours worked in excess of those normally rostered do attract overtime compensation; the rules on this are too complex to go into here. The long, anti-social and unpredictable hours are frequently a cause of domestic disharmony (there will be many missed birthdays, Christmas dinners and children's plays) and divorce amongst police officers is, regrettably, common.

Another cause of domestic strife is the officer's emotional state on getting home. Policing is, as you have seen, an occupation that generates a great deal of stress, frustration and other negative emotions, but while you are working, the need to be professional means that you have to keep your emotions under strict control. Therefore, there is the temp-tation to want to unload on your partner when you finally get home, at whatever hour of the day. If not done too often there is not generally a problem, but continually 'taking the job home' is a sure-fire way to make your partner extremely unhappy and to damage your relationship (wise police officers know this and will have developed a way of 'dumping work' before going home).

If you are serious about joining the police and are in a long-term rela-tionship you would be well advised to discuss what it is likely to mean for both of you and make sure that you are both happy to deal with it.

> 'The camaraderie. Whatever position I have had the fortune to have been
> in, there has always been a sense of team spirit, and, whenever problems
> have arisen, whether at work or at home, there has always been someone
> to talk to.'
> **PC in a county force**

7.2 **Dealing with Confrontation**

Dealing with confrontation is an everyday occurrence for every police officer. Getting people to do what you want them to do is a very large part of the job. There are an awful lot of people who will not want to oblige you and will tell you so, to the point of violence. There are also people who will hate you simply because of the uniform you are wearing.

It also needs to be stressed that policing can be an extremely hazard-ous and dangerous occupation where, regrettably, officers have died in the line of duty. A monument to fallen police officers can be found on the Mall in London, which is a reminder to all of the courage and ulti-mate sacrifice that people interested in joining the job sometimes forget about.

In Chapter 9 you will find out that you will be expertly trained in how to deal with confrontation and prove your competence in these skills before you are allowed out on the streets. However, make no mistake about it, there will be times when you will have to tell people directly what you want them to do and, if necessary, make them do it. You will be shouted at, sworn at and spat on and, regardless of the training you have received, you will very likely be assaulted. If you go into any police station in England and Wales you will not find anyone who has been an active police officer who has not been physically attacked on duty. Your training will reduce the frequency and, hopefully, lessen the potential seriousness, but you will be assaulted at some stage.

As with other things we have mentioned if you are not sure that you are prepared to deal with confrontation and violence then it will be best if you did not pursue a career in the police.

'...some days it's routine—some days it's anything but!'
PC in a county force

7.3 **Workload**

Even aside from the stress engendered when dealing with some individual incidents, the sheer volume of work, and the need to deliver results, places a lot of pressure on every police officer, whatever department they may be in. Although there have been several national and force projects to reduce the amount of bureaucracy and administration involved in policing, all officers will find themselves writing and filling in forms. Paperwork can add considerably to officers' workloads and is a common reason why some decide to leave the job. Being able to effectively manage your time will be one of the key skills that will either ensure you enjoy and get the most out of policing, or not.

'Managing a busy workload requires focus and commitment and a determination to deliver—this is not about performance targets, it's about providing the public we serve with the best possible service at a time when they need us the most. A quick phone call, email or simply dropping by to see a victim makes all the difference, and lets you see the people behind the paperwork.' **Sergeant in a large urban force**

7.4 **Why People Stay**

After changes to the terms and conditions of police service, officers will now work for 35 years to get full pension entitlements. However, there are opportunities to work for longer and some police officers may retire, but continue to work for the force as a police support staff member.

Policing is a job that relies on effective teamwork, and one element of this is that officers make friendships with colleagues and team members, which makes for a healthy and fulfilling workplace. Although some incidents may prove to be challenging or particularly upsetting, the strength of the Service is in its people and the support that is in place to give assistance.

Overall, resignations by police officers are very low, which indicates the sort of working experience that many have, even though it can be tough at times for individuals and families alike.

This chapter has not been written to put anybody off joining the police. Like the rest of the book, it is intended to inform potential police officers what 'The Job' is actually about and what doing it entails. It is much better for everybody if new recruits come in with their eyes wide open and knowing what to expect. The subject of joining the police is the focus of the next part of the book. There we will look at the recruiting process and the training new officers are given.

> 'Sometimes, when investigating a crime, something happens—a witness says something or the scientific people call and you know with a bit of effort you are going to win this one. You are spurred on and can't stop working. It's a brilliant feeling.'
> **Detective Inspector (20 years' service) in specialist investigations**

> 'A real sense of achievement, a simple thank you from a member of the public you have helped is worth its weight in gold.'
> **PC in a large city force**

PART III
RECRUITING AND TRAINING

8

THE SELECTION PROCESS

As you will probably have realised by now, if you did not know it already, being a police officer is not an easy job and it is not a job that a lot of people *can* do. There are about 8,000 recruits taken on across England and Wales each year; there are more than 50,000 applicants. You should not let that statistic put you off trying; a great many applications are turned down, not because the person did not have what it takes, but because they did not understand the recruiting system and so failed to demonstrate their potential for the job. In this chapter we will look at the selection process and how it works.

8.1 Would I Fit In?

Before we look at the process itself it will probably be useful to deal with a question asked by a great many people thinking of joining, 'Would I fit In?' As you will have seen from the previous chapters, policing deals with a wide variety of issues in the community—and it needs an equally wide variety of individuals to do it. If you think back to Peel's Principles of Policing that we looked at in Chapter 2, it was clearly set down that if the Service is to be effective then 'the police are the public and the public are the police' must be true; in other words the make-up of the force must reflect the make-up of the communities it serves. Whilst this has yet to be fully achieved, it is true to say that officers from all different cultural, social, religious and ethnic backgrounds train and work alongside each other.

In a report called 'Training Matters' (which we will meet formally in Chapter 9) Her Majesty's Inspector of Constabulary said:

Few other professions place so much importance on the way their members interact with customers and each other.

You should note the last phrase, 'and each other'. Teamwork is fundamental to modern policing and a fellow officer's background is irrelevant, all that matters is whether they can do the job.

Every police force has a well publicised equal opportunities policy that sets out the way in which individuals can expect to be treated. Of course, the strict legal requirements which make it unlawful to discriminate against anyone because of their sex, race, married status, age, religious belief, sexual orientation or any other inappropriate factor apply just as much to the police as any other job.

So the answer to the question 'Would I fit in?' is quite simple. Do you meet the minimum standards in relation to physical fitness, character and can you pass the selection process? If the answer to these questions is yes, then you could fit right in.

8.2 **The Paper Sift**

The first stage of the selection process is assessing the application forms; most applications that fail do so at this point.

There are three main reasons why some applicants who could make good police officers fail at this stage. The first reason is that they didn't fill in the application form in accordance with the instructions. It may sound obvious but, given the number of applicants who clearly don't, it has to be mentioned here; do read the guidance notes for completion before you start to fill the form in. Pay particular attention to the section on competency assessment.

The second reason is poor spelling, punctuation, grammar and general presentation. As it says in the notes, these are assessed throughout the form. If you make more than a couple of spelling mistakes your application will be rejected.

The third reason is that the applicant fails to demonstrate the skills and competencies that the process is looking for in the competency assessment section. This doesn't mean that they don't have them; simply that they didn't demonstrate them on the form. Unfortunately, confidentiality precludes details of how these questions are scored being included here but there are some things that can be said.

The questions that most people fall down on are the first four. Look at the headings of these:

> Q1 It is vitally important that police officers show respect for others, irrespective of their background.

> Q2 Police officers often work in teams and it is important that you are able to work well with others, and are willing to share in the less attractive jobs.

> Q3 Police officers often need to remain calm and act logically and decisively in very difficult circumstances.

> Q4 Police officers have to be able to communicate with a wide range of people, both verbally and in writing.

In each case you have to provide an example from your life relating to the topic. If you look you can see where the assessors are going, namely:

- Q1—respect for race and diversity;
- Q2—team working;
- Q3—resilience; and
- Q4—effective communication.

Furthermore when you look at the some of the questions, for each that you are asked to answer, you can see that they are also looking for evidence in relation to:

- personal responsibility;

- problem solving; and
- community and customer focus.

These seven things are the core behaviours that police officers are expected to have and to develop. It is worth looking at them in a little detail.

Respect for race and diversity

Understands other people's views and takes them into account. Is tactful and diplomatic when dealing with people. Treats people with dignity and respect at all times, no matter what their background, status, circumstances or appearance.

Team working

Works effectively as a team member and helps build relationships with the team. Actively helps and supports others to achieve team goals.

Resilience

Shows reliability and resilience in difficult circumstances. Remains calm and confident, and responds logically and decisively in difficult situations.

Effective communication

Communicates all needs, instructions and decisions clearly. Adapts the style of communication to meet the needs of the audience. Asks probing questions to check understanding.

Personal responsibility

Takes personal responsibility for own actions and for sorting out issues or problems that arise. Is focused on achieving results to required standards and developing skills and knowledge.

Problem solving

Gathers enough relevant information to understand specific issues and events. Uses information to identify problems and draw logical conclusions. Makes good decisions.

Community and customer focus

Provides a high level of service to customers. Maintains contact with customers, works out what they need and responds to them. Is aware of issues of diversity, and understands and is sensitive to cultural and racial differences.

Applicants who provide evidence to demonstrate the above behaviours don't fail the competency assessment. Of course, space is limited and you will not be able to show every trait from one example, but the more you can show the better. Armed with this information you may want to look at the sample answer given in the guidance notes and see how the author has worked in the core behaviours.

Meeting the requirements of the paper sift is not particularly difficult if you think about it and work out your answers carefully.

8.3 **The Assessment Centre**

When you are through the paper sift you will be invited to the next stage of the selection process, a one-day assessment centre. With your invitation will come an information pack which details how the day will run and, crucially, the competencies that will be tested—together with the positive and negative behaviour indicators for each (i.e. those things that the assessors are wanting to hear and those things that, if you produce too many of them, will result in your failing). Most, if not all, forces also provide a pre-event briefing for candidates. Make sure you read all the documents in the pack carefully and thoroughly before the day.

Experienced assessors have said that it is very unusual to fail the assessment centre if you prepare for it properly.

During the day you will take part in four assessed activities:

- a numerical reasoning test;
- a verbal reasoning/literacy test;
- an interview; and
- a series of four interactive role plays.

There is not much that can be said about the numerical reasoning test other than if you have Adult Level 2 or GCSE mathematics you should not have a problem with it. The others could usefully do with some detailed description here.

Literacy test

In this test you will be given a briefing sheet which details a problem. Your task is to draft a letter in response. As with the application form, clear, concise and grammatically correct English is a must. In particular if you make more than five spelling mistakes you will fail. Other than that a logical structure and a reasoned proposed course of action that addresses the problem should see you clear.

Interview

This interview will be like no other one you have ever had or, probably, ever will have. It lasts for 20 minutes and the single assessor will ask you four questions. He or she will read the questions from a script and each one will be prefixed by the competency that is being assessed. You will have five minutes to answer the question. During your answer the assessor will be listening for the behaviour indicators for the relevant competency and marking them on a score card, so they will not make any eye contact with you or give any sort of feedback (no nodding of the head or 'ah ha' noises that are part of everyday communication). If you come to the end of your answer before the five minutes is up the assessor may ask you if you have finished and if you have they will move on to the next question. On the other hand if you are still talking at the five-minute mark the assessor will cut you off and move on to the next question.

The reason for this unusual structure is to ensure that every candidate is treated exactly the same and so the process is as fair as it possibly can be. There is, however, no doubt that it can seem to be a cold and artificial way of conducting an interview. It is very difficult to talk to the top of someone's head, especially when you are getting no feedback from the person at all. It is not unknown for unprepared candidates to dry up after a sentence or two for each answer and then they and the assessor have to sit in silence until the 20 minutes is up.

The information pack will tell you what competencies will be tested and what the positive behaviour indictors are. So, well before the day, for each competency, think of two examples from any part of your life (work, home, school, university, armed services—it doesn't matter) and rehearse them. Even go so far as to write down what you are going to say and learn it by heart. Make sure that you check your lines against the behaviour indicators. Then in the interview listen for the competency to be tested in the question and explain *both* your prepared examples for it—always give two examples, that way you can cover more of the behaviours.

The only other thing to remember is, especially if the question is about teamwork, don't say 'we', always say 'I'; it is you that is being assessed not the team.

The interview might be cold and artificial but, if you have prepared for it, it is the easiest of the activities.

Interactive role play

You will do four interactive role plays, or, if you prefer, role exercises. At every assessment centre held so far they have been based around a fictional shopping centre and the candidate plays the role of the customer services manager—there is no reason to suspect that this will change in the future. You start at the preparation station for your first exercise. There you will find a briefing sheet and you will have five minutes to read it; you are allowed to make notes. At the end of five minutes a buzzer will sound and you will move to the door of the actual event. After 90 seconds the buzzer will sound again and in you go. Inside will be a role actor—the person that is mentioned in the briefing—and standing in the corner behind you, and out of your line of view, will be the assessor (there may occasionally be a third person present: this will be an external verifier who is there to check the work of the assessor, so ignore them). The role actor will give you the first line and you have five minutes to deal with the situation, whatever it may be. At the end of that time the buzzer will go again and the actor will immediately stop talking, the assessment will be over and you will move on to the preparation station for the next exercise.

The role actor has a briefing; it will tell him or her the demeanour that he or she is to take (nervous, arrogant, angry, etc.) and the 14 lines he or she is allowed to say. No matter what you say, or how the situation develops, they will never say anything other than one of those 14 lines.

Some people find role plays difficult and, unlike the interview, there is not a lot you can do in preparation. If this applies to you, then you might want to think about where and how you could practise getting into a role and behaving the way you would if you were a customer services manager of a shopping centre. It will be fatal to your chances of success if you walked into the room and had an attack of the giggles or otherwise didn't start demonstrating your competencies straight away—you need to fill the five minutes with quality.

As ever, competencies are being tested in this activity and you will need to show the behaviour traits. Good people fail here not because they can't do it but because they don't show what is being looked for. To give an example, if the competency being assessed is problem solving you will need to show that you gather information to understand the problem, consider possible options that logically follow from the information you have gathered and then choose one that makes some sort of sense to the assessor. If you merely listen to the problem and then announce a solution you will score very badly, no matter how good your solution is.

Other points to remember are:

- listen to the actor, really listen to what they say;
- do not use jargon, particularly police jargon;
- do not try to deal with the situation as if you were a police officer;
- ignore the assessor;
- when you have finished a role play, wipe it from your mind;
- never point your finger at the actor or use other confrontational or inappropriate body language—you will fail if you do.

To finish this section on the assessment centre, there are some general points that may be of use. First of all your behaviour is monitored all of the time and not just in the assessed activities. You will instantly fail if:

- you use inappropriate language (racist or sexist comments, etc.);
- your conduct in any activity is hopelessly wide of the mark;
- you talk so softly or indistinctly you cannot be heard or understood;
- your communication makes no sense.

There is no dress code for the assessment centre; how you look forms no part of the assessment. However, one of the things that most definitely will be tested is your ability to communicate effectively. When we are talking, the listener only gets 7 per cent of the message from what we actually say; another 35 per cent comes from how we say it and the rest—the majority—comes from our body language. How you are dressed is part of that body language. The only thing that will be scored is what you say (the 7 per cent). However, the assessors are only human and your appearance will have a subconscious impact and that *may* affect your score and that *may* mean the difference between pass and fail.

For each activity the assessor will have something that looks like a large version of the form you fill in when buying a national lottery ticket. On it will be a line for each behaviour trait for the competency being tested; for each trait you will be marked on whether you demonstrate it and if so how well. At the end of the assessment centre your score cards will be sent to a national centre where they will be computer marked together with all the candidates from across the country and a standardised score will be produced. You will be sent your result two weeks after the assessment centre.

8.4 **The Fitness Test**

If you pass the assessment centre the last hurdle (other than the medical and reference checks, which needn't detain us here) is the fitness test. A lot of applicants worry about this, but unless they are grossly unfit they shouldn't. It is nowhere near as hard as people think—indeed, to prove a point, a sergeant in his 40s recently successfully completed it whilst smoking a cigarette. The fitness test consists of three activities:

- the shuttle run;
- the push test; and
- the pull test.

In the shuttle run, candidates must run up and down a 15 metre track for at least a set time (currently three and half minutes for men and two minutes forty-five seconds for women). Each 15 metre run must be completed before a buzzer sounds; as the test goes on, the interval between buzzes gets progressively shorter, so the candidate must run faster.

The push and pull tests are done sitting at a machine. The candidate has three goes at pulling a spring-loaded bar towards him or her and three goes at pushing it away. A meter built into the machine records the strength of the push and pull and for each at least one of the three attempts must reach a certain level. However, the pass mark is sufficiently low that a normal, averagely fit adult can achieve it without too much difficulty.

The statistics indicate that getting into the Service is not easy—only about 15 per cent of applicants are successful. However, as you have seen, providing you actually have the personal attributes that are being sought, some sound preparation at each stage will reduce the odds dramatically. Of course, getting in is only the start; you also have to complete the training successfully and we will look at what that means in the next chapter.

FURTHER READING

→ <http://www.policecouldyou.co.uk>—Police Service recruitment website.
→ H. Tolley, C. Tolley, B. Hodge, *How to Pass the New Police Selection System*, 2004, Kogan Page.
→ S. Sutcliffe & W. Francis, *Passing the Police Recruit Assessment Process*, 2007, Law Matters Publishing.

9

INITIAL TRAINING

Once you have got through the selection process you will be sent a letter offering you an appointment to your force. It is usually somewhere around three to eighteen months before you actually begin your new career, but that day will eventually come when you turn up at the force headquarters or training centre to start learning how to do 'The Job'. In this chapter we will look at the sort of training you will receive and how you will be assessed.

First of all a note of caution: as you have seen there are more than 40 police forces in England and Wales and despite the standardisation that has been going on over recent years they are all proudly unique and have their own traditions and, in particular, they do not all use the same terminology. In this book we try to use only standard terms, but don't be surprised if, when you talk to individual forces, they use different names for the roles, tasks and processes that you will read about below.

9.1 Student Officer

The first thing to note about initial police training is that it extends for a two-year period and during that time you will be a student officer. The term 'probationer' is now no longer used, but this initial two-year period may still be referred to as your 'probation' period of assessment.

Having recalled our discussion in Chapter 4, you will probably remember that it will be your task to prove that you can do 'The Job'. We will look at what that means in practice later on, when we consider how you will be assessed during your training, but right now there is a very important fact you need to know about—it is called 'Regulation 13'.

We saw in Chapter 1 that as a constable you will not have a contract of employment and at least some employment law will not apply to you. Instead your life on duty and off will be governed by the Code of Conduct and Police Regulations. Whilst you are on probation Regulation 13 is important. What it says is:

> . . . during his period of probation in the force the services of a constable may be dispensed with at any time if the chief officer considers that he is not fitted, physically or mentally, to perform the duties of his office, or that he is not likely to become an efficient or well conducted constable.

What this means is that if your conduct (on duty or off) or your performance is unacceptable you can be fired. Probationers have been sacked for dishonest behaviour that, in other occupations, probably would not even merit a written warning. Drunken behaviour off-duty, particularly when it is likely to bring discredit on the force, has also seen a fair number of probationers face dismissal under this regulation. A bad sickness record could, quite likely, lead the force to decide that the officer is physically unsuited to 'The Job' and to dismiss him or her. However, failing to meet the standards required in training is the biggest cause of Regulation 13 being invoked.

You should not be unduly alarmed about this regulation; no force wants to lose people in whom, even during their early training, they have invested considerable sums. Except in cases of unacceptable conduct, Regulation 13 is never used without warning. Officers who are struggling will always be given lots of help and support, but at the end of the day there is no room for someone who cannot meet the grade. There is no appeal to an employment tribunal for a dismissal under Regulation 13, though the officer can apply to the courts for a judicial review of the decision.

9.2 **Initial Police Learning and Development Programme**

The Initial Police Learning and Development Programme (IPLDP) is the national standard for the training of new officers during their first two years of training and was introduced across England and Wales in April 2006.

Previously, initial training had followed the same path since at least the end of World War II. After a short induction period at their Force Training School, recruits were sent off to a District Training Centre for a residential course lasting 12 weeks (the course had been as short as 10 weeks and as long as 15). There, in company with recruits from other forces in the region, they were schooled in the basics of law and procedure, with role play exercises carried out on site to enable them to practise their new skills and knowledge.

On returning to their force the recruits went through a local procedure course intended to get them up to speed with their own force's way of doing things. Then they went to their stations and worked with an experienced constable who would tutor them for up to 10 weeks, before finally being released to work on their own. Short training courses were attended during the remainder of the two years to deliver more new law knowledge and refresh what they had learned at the District Training Centre.

On the whole this training regime worked reasonably well and was enjoyed by just about everyone involved. However, it did have some serious weaknesses and as the years wore on these were becoming more and more apparent. What had been ideal in the 1940s, and more than acceptable in the 1970s, was, by the mid-1990s, struggling. Society had changed dramatically since 1946 and not only had society's expectations of the police changed with it, so too had the needs of the recruits.

9.3 **Current Training Regime**

As the current training regime has some minimum standards but otherwise allows forces to implement a training programme that best suits their own needs and the needs of the communities they serve, you will by now have guessed that, with over 40 forces, there are over 40 different training programmes. Therefore, it is impossible to be exact about the training that you will undergo. What we can do is look at the mandatory features that will be common to all and look at the different styles of training that are on offer.

National Occupational Standards

To ensure that every officer, no matter what force they join, achieves a minimum standard of capability to do the job, all student officers must demonstrate competence in 22 National Occupational Standards (NOSs).

National Occupational Standards have been developed by the Skills for Justice agency in conjunction with representatives from ACPO, police authorities and community partners. They provide a method of assessing competent performance in terms of the tasks to be achieved in the workplace.

Each of the 22 standards has one or more elements which in turn have specific tasks—competence in which must be demonstrated (known as performance criteria). This may sound complex but, once you get the hang of it, it is actually quite straightforward. We will look at how the assessment of competence is done later on in this chapter. There is not the space in this book to set down the relevant NOSs but you can find them on the Skills for Justice website (<http://www.skillsforjustice.net/nos/with-ple.htm>).

Stages: basic training and independent patrol

The time a student officer spends on probation is divided into two parts, the basic training period and independent patrol.

Basic training is the period when new officers learn the fundamental skills and knowledge that will enable them to perform street duty on their own; in the next section we will look at what this involves. The length of time that this period of learning takes varies from force to force, the shortest would appear to be 26 weeks and the longest is 52 weeks. Before officers can be signed off to work on their own, they have to show that they are competent in 11 key areas of day-to-day policing. This list of competencies is known as the Police Action Checklist (PAC).

Once they have been granted independent patrol, student officers join an operational section in the police station to which they have been posted and work as a regular member of the team. In this time they will continue to show their competence against the 22 NOSs and must, by the end of the two years, have all of them signed off. They will, generally, also undergo periods of additional formal training, which in some forces includes local university attendance. The amount of time that is devoted to this seems to depend on the length of the basic training and it varies from more than six weeks to none at all.

One interesting thing to note about police training is that student officers on independent patrol, although they have not finished their training, much less shown that they are competent in all the areas necessary for a fully fledged police officer, are treated just like any other regular PC. They are sent to calls as they come in and are expected, at least by the public, to cope with whatever the job throws at them. One officer on her very first day out on her own was the first at the scene of a stranger-rape and had to deal with the situation, the scene and a very distressed victim for a considerable period before more experienced help could get there.

Key elements

However a force organises its basic training and however long it takes it will contain some key elements and we will look at these now.

Induction

The training will start with an induction period. This will probably be quite short and is designed to introduce you to the force and the training programme. You will be issued with your uniform (and taught how to wear it) and your warrant card as well as being 'sworn in' as a constable (remember the attestation in Chapter 1).

Classroom learning

Student officers have to learn a great deal of law, policy and procedure. Although some of this can and will be absorbed in the workplace, there is no substitute for a safe learning environment. In most cases the training will be delivered by experienced police officers who hold recognised training qualifications. In some forces, especially those who are working in partnership with a university, some of the training is carried out by lecturers who have the specialist knowledge required. Regardless of who is delivering it, you will find that in modern police training there are very few old-fashioned chalk-and-talk lessons. Sessions are designed to be interactive and to ensure that all students learn as much as they can.

In most forces the classroom learning takes place on police premises, usually the force training school, but others have their student officers on a university campus integrated with the wider student community. In all but one or two forces, basic training is not residential and the classroom element takes place during the normal working day—that is to say nine to five from Monday to Friday.

Officer safety training

Officer safety training is about the skills, both verbal and physical, necessary to deal with violent conflict with the least chance of getting hurt and using the minimum force necessary. This training includes how to use a baton and handcuffs properly and the correct use of incapacitant spray. All officers are required to qualify in these skills before they can set foot on the street as an operational officer.

Workplace learning

Workplace learning, sometimes called supervised patrol, is when the new officer takes to the streets in the company of a tutor constable to put into practice the knowledge and skills learned in the classroom and to learn more, both directly and indirectly. In some forces this takes place in one continuous block at the end of a lengthy period of classroom based training; in others, periods in the classroom and periods in the workplace are interleaved and the activities in the latter are carefully directed to help achieve set learning outcomes. During this phase of your training you can expect to be working something close to the normal shift pattern of either the response team or NPT you are attached to.

Community placements

One of the problems identified with the old style of initial police training was that it all took place in a closed police environment and new officers did not learn about the communities they were to police. Now all officers are required to spend a minimum of 80 hours in community placements. Depending on the needs of the force, this time can be spent in short visits to learn something of community customs and needs (for example, a day spent with the imam at a local mosque) and/or longer periods actually working in and with a community group (for example, a needle exchange scheme).

Community placements are being seen as successful in helping to break down barriers between the police and some parts of society and also improving the officers' abilities to police sensitively, taking into account the needs of individuals.

Valuing diversity and promoting equality

We have mentioned the subject of race and diversity on several occasions already, but it is so fundamental to good policing that it forms a core part of your training.

The subject of diversity is not about political correctness, it is about being able to police more effectively, more easily and, from your point of view, more enjoyably. You will learn the full reasons why this should be so in your training, but at the heart of your diversity training will be the need to treat everyone as an individual and according to their needs. If you reflect on the ideas we have been discussing you may well see why that makes sense for them, 'The Job' and for you.

To complete your training you will have to show competence in a specific National Occupational Standard relating to diversity. It is number AA1, Promote Equality and Value Diversity. Incidentally this standard is now mandatory for everyone working in the Justice Sector, not just police officers.

Assessment

As a student officer you have to demonstrate your competence to do 'The Job'. If you don't, as we have seen, you will lose your job. This simple fact is at the heart of the assessment process—the student must prove themselves. To ensure that this process is fair and open each student officer will keep a portfolio of evidence as they progress through their training. In most forces this is known as the SOLAP or Student Officer Learning Assessment Portfolio, and if you have ever worked for an NVQ you will be quite at home with the process.

To prove competence in a PAC or NOS the student has to produce evidence. This can be in the form of a witness testament from a qualified officer who saw the student demonstrate the required behaviour or it can be documents which in themselves show what is required (in some cases the SOLAP will only contain a reference number as the original document will be of operational importance—for example, a crime file). On a regular basis each student's SOLAP will be examined by a qualified assessor and if they agree that evidence is sufficient the relevant performance criteria will be signed off in the SOLAP. The work of the assessor will subsequently be checked by one or more qualified verifiers to ensure standards are maintained and equal across the force area. Just so you know, the work of the verifier will be dip-checked by an external verifier to ensure that standards across forces are equal.

In addition to the evidence for the NOSs the SOLAP will contain a record of the student's assessment against theoretical knowledge; that is to say, how well they know the law, policies and procedure that they have been required to learn. Whilst the assessment of NOSs is standardised across England and Wales, how the students' theoretical knowledge is measured varies from force to force. Some use formal examinations (generally of the multiple-choice style), some use essays and written projects, some use a mixture of both.

The SOLAP will also contain notes of tutorial meetings and such action plans as are agreed to help the student officer develop. Finally, it will contain a learning diary or reflective journal.

Qualifications

Some forces have entered into partnership arrangements with a local university, and the completion of basic training (i.e. achieving independent patrol) will lead to the award of a Certificate in Higher Education—the equivalent of the first year of an honours degree course. Of these forces, some offer student officers the opportunity to study for and achieve a Foundation Degree before they finish probation, and at least one force insists that they do.

The key point to remember about initial police training is that it is really about getting you up to the standards that are needed. There is no sudden death. If, when you submit your SOLAP, the assessor does not agree that you have sufficient evidence for a particular performance criterion, it is not an instant fail. They will tell you why and what you need to do. This is not a pass or fail process, it is a developmental process. Nobody will expect you to do the job perfectly first time out, your senior officers will expect you to make mistakes and get it wrong. The only time this becomes a problem (and so leads to Regulation 13) is when you don't learn from your mistakes.

FURTHER READING

→ <http://www.policecouldyou.co.uk>—Police Service recruitment website.

→ <http://www.skillsforjustice.com>—Government skills website for the Police Service.

PART IV
POLICING POWERS

10

HUMAN RIGHTS AND POLICE POWERS

If you look back to the very beginning of this book at the attestation you will be required to take on becoming a constable, you will see that a significant part of your duty in the office is to 'uphold fundamental human rights'. You may well have heard or read a lot of stories in the media over recent years about how this duty has been discharged both within the Service and by other government agencies. Human rights are a fundamental part of every officer's obligations, in this chapter we will look at what is really meant by them and how they influence every aspect of policing.

10.1 The European Convention on Human Rights

In the aftermath of World War II the countries of Western Europe decided that some guarantee was required to ensure that the horrors and abuses perpetrated by some during that conflict could never be repeated. The result was, to give it its full title, 'The European Convention for the Protection of Human Rights and Fundamental Freedoms'.

The Convention was drafted with a very large input by the British Government of the day and was signed by all the countries in the Council of Europe in 1959 as a treaty legally binding on all of them. Thus the protection of fundamental human rights is neither new nor something that has been imposed on the UK as part of its obligations as a member of the European Union (EU). That said, all members of the EU, including those from the former communist states, have now signed the treaty.

What is much more recent is the Human Rights Act 1998. Until this piece of legislation, the British Government and all its agencies were bound to uphold the human rights of its citizens, but if someone had a grievance they had to go to the European Court of Human Rights in Strasbourg to have their case heard—something very few people did. What the Act did was to integrate the Convention into UK law, thus allowing its citizens to seek redress through the UK courts. It also—and this makes it a very significant Act, particularly for police officers—insists that all other laws must be interpreted *and applied* so as to be compliant with the Convention. Notably all laws, courts and legal proceedings in England and Wales must be compliant with people's rights under the Convention.

10.2 Public Authorities

The aim of the Convention, and thus the Human Rights Act 1998, was to protect the individual from the State; it says nothing about relations between private individuals.

So what does the Act class as the State? The term used is 'public authority'. Whether a body is a public authority or not will be determined by the type of work or function that it carries out. Some are obvious, for example: government departments, local authorities, the courts, the fire and ambulance services and, of course, the police. All public authorities, and all the people working for them, have to pay due regard to people's rights under the Convention when exercising *all and any* of their functions. It is very important that you note that not only will your force be bound by the Act, but you as an individual have a duty in law.

10.3 The Convention Rights

One of the reasons that our rights and, as police officers, obligations under the Convention went without much notice for so long was that they were pretty much those freedoms which we have been fortunate enough to enjoy in the UK for a very long time. If you think about those things which make up a truly free country, the basic rights that you would want for yourself, your family and your friends, most of them are covered in the Convention. In fact some are so fundamental that we have taken them for granted for centuries—like the right to liberty and freedom of speech.

Once in the Police Service you will not be required to learn the Articles and Protocols of the Convention, but you will need to know what they say in general terms. The rights and protocols are summarised below.

Obligation to respect human rights (Article 1)

This simply binds those countries which sign the Convention to abide by its terms.

Right to life (Article 2)

Everyone's right to life shall be protected by law.

Freedom from torture (Article 3)

No one shall be subjected to torture or to inhuman or degrading treatment.

Freedom from slavery and forced labour (Article 4)

No one shall be held in slavery or servitude. No one shall be required to perform forced or compulsory labour.

Right to liberty and security (Article 5)

Everyone has the right to liberty and security of person. No one shall be deprived of his or her liberty, save in accordance with a procedure prescribed by law.

Everyone who is arrested shall be informed promptly, in a language which he or she understands, of the reasons for his or her arrest and of any charge against him or her.

Everyone arrested or detained shall be brought promptly before a judge or other officer and shall be entitled to a trial within a reasonable time or to be released pending trial.

Right to a fair trial (Article 6)

In the determination of his or her civil rights and obligations or of any criminal charge against him or her, everyone is entitled to a fair and public hearing within a reasonable time by an independent and impartial tribunal established by law.

Everyone charged with a criminal offence shall be presumed innocent until proven guilty.

No punishment without crime (Article 7)

No one shall be held guilty of any criminal offence on account of any act or omission which did not constitute a criminal offence under national or international law at the time when it was committed.

Right to private life (Article 8)

Everyone has the right to respect for his or her private and family life, home and correspondence.

Freedom of thought (Article 9)

Everyone has the right to freedom of thought, conscience and religion.

Freedom of expression (Article 10)

Everyone has the right to freedom of expression.

Freedom of assembly and association (Article 11)

Everyone has the right to freedom of peaceful assembly and to freedom of association with others, including the right to form and to join trade unions for the protection of his or her interests.

Right to marry (Article 12)

Men and women of marriageable age have the right to marry, and to found a family, according to the laws of that State.

Prohibition of discrimination in Convention rights (Article 14)

The enjoyment of rights and freedoms set forth in this Convention shall be secured without discrimination on any ground such as sex, race, colour, language, religion, association with a national minority, property, birth or other status.

Protection of property (Protocol 1, Article 1)

Every natural or legal person is entitled to the peaceful protection of their possessions.

Right to education (Protocol 1, Article 2)

No person shall be denied the right to education.

Right to free elections (Protocol 1, Article 3)

The parties [to the Convention] undertake to hold free elections at reasonable intervals by secret ballot, under conditions which will ensure free expression of the opinion of the people.

There should have been no surprises; the rights are probably no more or less than you would expect.

You may have noticed the absence of an Article 13, the reason for its absence here is that it deals with the right to an effective remedy when your other rights are breached. It is not specifically mentioned in the Human Rights Act 1998, not least because that Act in itself provides the means for the inclusion of such remedies with national law.

The rights and freedoms set out above are universal, that is they apply to everyone in England and Wales. However, if you think about them for a few minutes you will see that the exercise of one person's individual rights might well impact on the rights and freedoms of another, indeed they might be in direct conflict. These are practical issues of great importance, especially to you as a police officer, so let us give them some consideration.

10.4 Balancing Competing Rights and Needs

The first thing to note is that our rights under the Convention come in two types. Some are *absolute*. That means that there is no room for debate, no watering down of their protection; infringement of them is prohibited—full stop. The right to freedom from torture (under Article 3) is an example of an absolute right. Other rights can be limited or restricted if necessary in certain circumstances in order to allow society to function. These are known as *qualified* rights. A good example would be the right to freedom of expression. Article 9 allows us to think what we like and Article 10 gives us the freedom to express those thoughts, but what if those thoughts are, for example, grossly offensive to another person? Similarly there are frequently occasions where the rights of an individual will conflict with the needs of the general public—the right to freedom of assembly against the need to allow people to go about their business, for instance. Very often the police have to balance these rights when making decisions on the streets. Sometimes this is done by senior officers (for example, in allowing demonstrations to take place in certain areas), but frequently it will be down to police officers on the ground to make a decision then and there.

The Convention recognised that there would be a need for the police, courts, local authorities and others to balance the expression or use of qualified rights and so many of its Articles include relevant limitations or exceptions. Although different ones apply to different Articles, three key features need to be considered when making decisions about balancing rights—the 'three tests'.

10.5 The Three Tests

Where the Convention gives individuals particular rights, any limitation of them will be carefully examined and must be cautiously applied. If this were not the case our rights could be overridden by any number of 'get out' clauses introduced by an unscrupulous State. Therefore, in very general terms, any limitations on rights conferred by the Convention must be:

- prescribed in law;
- intended to achieve a legitimate objective; *and*
- necessary and proportionate.

Let us look at these more closely.

Test 1: Prescribed by law

This means that there must be some clearly published law passed by the nation's normal process which allows the restriction on individuals' rights. Acts of Parliament that grant the police powers of arrest would be good examples of something that meets the first test.

Under the Human Rights Act 1998 the relevant government minister must certify that any proposed new law is compatible with our rights under the Convention. This is designed to ensure that no government is able to circumvent the Convention by simply introducing national laws which abrogate rights and freedoms conferred by it. You should note that such ministerial certificates can, and no doubt will, be challenged in the courts and the courts can and have declared that certain laws are incompatible with the Convention—forcing the government to change them.

Such safeguards ensure that our laws are compatible with the Convention, but this still does not control the way in which such laws are *used*. An example would be police powers of arrest. The officer might have a certain power given to him or her by law in accordance with the Convention. However, the way in which he or she uses that power is also of critical importance; hence the reason for test 2.

Test 2: Intended to achieve a legitimate objective

The purpose of this test is to ensure that the powers that are prescribed by laws satisfying test 1 are being *used* for the right reason. This second test ensures that, for example, just because the police have the power to arrest people and search their property, such powers are used only when in the proper discharge of their duties. Another example would be the misuse of official data. As a police officer you are entitled to view information on the owners of motor cars, but only as is necessary for you to do your job—looking up the details of a car you were thinking of buying would be a breach of the Convention. This second test is still not sufficient to ensure that individual rights and freedoms are properly protected, so we have the further safety net of test 3.

Test 3: Necessary and proportionate

Any actions that interfere with an individual's rights under the Convention must be 'necessary and proportionate to the end that is to be achieved'. Even though you may have a legal power granted by an Act of Parliament that passes test 1 and you use it to achieve a legitimate objective (passing test 2), your behaviour must not be over the top and heavy-handed. To satisfy test 3 you will need to be able to show that when you exercised that power it was *necessary* to do so and you were not doing more than you needed to. We will come back to the necessity test when we look at powers of arrest in the next chapter.

The important things to remember from this chapter are:

- Is there a public authority involved? As a police officer you have a positive duty to ensure rights are upheld, as will all your colleagues in the wider police family.
- Some rights under the Convention are limited in some way—if in doubt, check the wording of the individual Article.
- If you are thinking about any interference with a right under the Convention, apply the three tests to see how a court may look at the situation.
- Human rights is not an area of law that exists on its own—it touches every aspect of law, whether that be police powers, the laws of evidence or the wording of criminal offences themselves.

As you look at police law and procedure in the remainder of this book, and especially when you go on to study them in your training, keep these principles in mind—it's surprising where they crop up.

FURTHER READING

→ <http://www.opsi.gov.uk>. The Office of Public Sector Information is a site well worth becoming familiar with. Using its search function will give you access to all sorts of useful information, including all the Acts of Parliament.

11

POWERS OF ARREST

As you saw in Part I, police officers and their colleagues are entrusted with many powers and privileges over and above those granted to their fellow citizens. The most important of these powers, both practically and constitutionally, are those that enable them to deprive their fellow citizens of their liberty and to take possession of their property—powers of arrest, search and seizure.

It is essential that all police officers use their powers wisely, fairly and properly. Not only must they keep in mind the human rights issues, but they must also remember that improper use of powers can lead to individual officers being liable in both the civil and criminal courts and under internal disciplinary procedures. It can also lead to evidence being inadmissible and the criminal being allowed to get away with their crime. Perhaps even more importantly, the way officers use their powers does have a direct effect on the confidence that the community has in the police. Even when police officers exercise their powers lawfully, their actions can be perceived as a source of oppression and discrimination, leading to a lack of confidence and the creation of an atmosphere of distrust.

So what is an 'arrest'? If you were forced to come up with a definition you might say that it was taking someone to a police station against their will, and that would not be a bad summary. An arrest generally involves stopping someone from going where they please, by force if *necessary* in connection with an allegation of a criminal offence that has, or is suspected of having, taken place.

In modern times a distinction in law has been made between *arrest* and *detention*. The police have many powers to detain people short of arresting them. When you stop a motorist whilst controlling traffic you are, in effect, stopping them going about their business in a way that they may wish; but generally speaking the use of the word *detention* is reserved for more formal occasions. An example would be to detain someone for the purpose of a search or, under the Football (Disorder) Act 2000, a police officer may detain someone who has been banned from attending matches so as to stop them from travelling to a game.

It is important to keep the issues of arrest and detention as separate in your mind as they are in law, not least because, as any police officer will tell you, with an arrest comes a whole host of responsibilities and powers that do not follow if someone has merely been detained.

So, although arrests are usually made in connection with a criminal offence that has already taken place, occasionally they may be made for other reasons such as:

- to *prevent* something taking place (such as a breach of the peace);
- to take DNA samples or fingerprints;
- to return someone to prison who is unlawfully at large or to bring them before a court.

Usually a person is arrested because the officer suspects that they have done something wrong. However, there are also occasions when someone may be arrested because they:

- are about to do something wrong;
- might do something wrong unless they are arrested;
- have *not* done something that they were lawfully required to do (for example, a motorist who failed to provide a breath test when lawfully required to do so).

It is very important that you realise that, although an officer may have the power to arrest someone, it does not mean he or she has to. We will come back to this point later, but for now remember two things:

1. There is no general duty to arrest even when there is a power to do so; alternatives should always be considered.

2. An arrest is an exercise of personal responsibility. It is your power, your decision and you will have to be able to justify what you did—possibly in front of a judge. Nobody can order you to make an arrest except a court.

11.1 Lawful Arrests

Every arrest must be lawful—otherwise it is unlawful. This may sound like a very obvious statement, but it is extremely important. The person carrying out the arrest—like anyone using any legal power—*must* be able to point to some legal authority which allows them to do it. When you bring your prisoner before the custody officer you are going to have to justify your actions then and there. You will have to say why and for what offence you have arrested the person, and from that will be judged whether or not you had a power and why the arrest was necessary. The power to arrest may come from the following sources:

- the circumstances at the time;
- the provisions of a particular Act;
- an order of a court.

Powers that come from a court are easy to deal with; the court issues a warrant telling you who to arrest and you do it. The police powers that you need to worry about are those granted by various Acts of Parliament that you can exercise without reference to anybody else. These are described as powers of arrest *without warrant.*

Most (but by no means all) police powers of arrest, search and seizure come from one particular Act—the Police and Criminal Evidence Act 1984, more commonly known as PACE. Although it was passed more than 20 years ago, PACE has been regularly amended and updated, particularly by the Serious Organised Crime and Police Act 2005 (SOCPA).

11.2 **The Power to Arrest**

Until January of 2006 the powers of arrest without warrant for a constable were complex, however, since the provisions of section 110 of the SOCPA were introduced, policing powers seem, at first sight, to be much simpler.

The effect of this section is to modernise the powers of arrest for police officers, so first let's look at what PACE says.

Section 24 Arrest without warrant: Constables

(1) A constable may arrest without a warrant—

  (a) anyone who is about to commit an offence;

  (b) anyone who is in the act of committing an offence;

  (c) anyone whom he has reasonable grounds for suspecting to be about to commit an offence;

  (d) anyone whom he has reasonable grounds for suspecting to be committing an offence.

(2) If a constable has reasonable grounds for suspecting that an offence has been committed, he may arrest without a warrant anyone whom he has reasonable grounds to suspect of being guilty of it.

(3) If an offence has been committed, a constable may arrest without a warrant—

  (a) anyone who is guilty of the offence;

  (b) anyone whom he has reasonable grounds for suspecting to be guilty of it.

As a constable, you may now arrest anyone who you reasonably suspect is about to commit or is committing or has committed *any* offence. Yes, that's right, *any* offence; from dropping litter to murder, and even failing to ensure a child is wearing a seat belt in the back seat of a car.

(4) But the power of summary arrest conferred by subsection (1), (2) or (3) is exercisable only if the constable has reasonable grounds for believing that for any of the reasons mentioned in subsection (5) it is necessary to arrest the person in question.

(5) The reasons are—

   (a) to enable the name of the person in question to be ascertained (in the case where the constable does not know, and cannot readily ascertain, the person's name, or has reasonable grounds for doubting whether a name given by the person as his name is his real name);

   (b) correspondingly as regards the person's address;

   (c) to prevent the person in question—

     (i) causing physical injury to himself or any other person;

     (ii) suffering physical injury;

     (iii) causing loss of or damage to property;

     (iv) committing an offence against public decency (subject to subsection (6)); or

     (v) causing an unlawful obstruction of the highway;

   (d) to protect a child or other vulnerable person from the person in question;

   (e) to allow the prompt and effective investigation of the offence or of the conduct of the person in question;

   (f) to prevent any prosecution for the offence from being hindered by the disappearance of the person in question.

(6) Subsection (5)(c)(iv) applies only where members of the public going about their normal business cannot reasonably be expected to avoid the person in question.

This is the 'necessity test' which keeps police powers of arrest in line with the European Convention on Human Rights. In short what the law says is that a police officer can now arrest anybody on reasonable suspicion that they are about to commit, are committing or have committed any offence as long as it is *necessary* to do so.

    Whether you had reasonable suspicion or belief is always a matter for the courts to decide. The key word is reasonable. You must always be able to state the facts and information that you had at the time and why they gave rise to the suspicion or belief on which you based your decision. The court will decide whether, on the facts as given and in the circumstances of the case, an ordinary person *could* have come to the same conclusions as the officer. Again this illustrates the fact that a police officer must always be prepared to justify their decisions based on fact and law.

11.3 Tell Them What is Happening

Whenever a person is arrested and for whatever reason, the law (PACE) makes it very clear that the person must be told that they are under arrest and why—even if it should be obvious to them. The only exception is where the person escapes before the officer could give them the information.

It is an added requirement to make sure that the arrested person is given the information in a language that they understand. This is particularly important if you have arrested someone whose first language is not English or who has a serious hearing impairment (in which case you'll need to get hold of a competent signer as soon as possible after the arrest). The other thing you have to tell people when they are arrested, or about to be questioned about an offence, is the caution.

11.4 A Word of Caution

Before worrying about the exact wording of the caution, you should note that it is the principle behind it that is the most important thing. The idea is to alert the person who is being arrested, or is to be questioned, of their right not to say anything and to warn them that anything they say may be used in evidence against them in court. It is also a warning that by not saying anything they may be harming any defence which they later use in court. The actual wording of the caution has been designed to get this message across in the simplest way possible and it has been carefully written to make it as easy as possible for everyone.

12

STOP AND SEARCH

In addition to their powers of arrest, another important power given to the police is the power to stop and search people and vehicles. This is probably the most controversial of police powers and it is essential that all officers have a full understanding, not only of what powers they have, but when, where and how they should be used.

By this time there is probably no need to say where the powers come from—it is the Police and Criminal Evidence Act 1984 (PACE) Code A. PACE also has Codes of Practice to help people interpret its provisions and set guidelines to be followed. There are also powers under the Terrorism Act 2000 to carry out stop and search, but as an initial guide this chapter will concentrate on powers under PACE.

12.1 **Where?**

Generally, a police officer may use the power to stop and search in public places. This will include places that are open to the public on payment (for example, museums, cinemas and sports stadiums). It does not include people's homes or any attached land. However, if a person that an officer wishes to search is in a garden which is part of a house, the power to search may be used provided that the officer has *reasonable grounds for believing* that the person does not live there *and* that they are not in the garden with the permission of someone who does live there. If you think about it this makes sense; whilst it would be unreasonable to routinely search people in their own gardens, it is necessary for the police to have a power to stop and search people who are in someone else's garden—as burglars often are!

These restrictions relate to where the person to be searched must have been found. You do not have to carry out the search in the same place. In fact for some detailed and thorough searches the person should be taken out of public view.

12.2 **What?**

You may search any person, any vehicle and anything that is in or on the vehicle (luggage, roof boxes, tool kits, etc.). You may search for stolen or prohibited articles, the latter generally being weapons or tools for use in the course of a crime. The power to search includes a power to detain the person for '*as long as is reasonably necessary*' for the search to be carried out.

12.3 **When?**

Before an officer can use their power to stop and search someone they must have 'reasonable grounds for suspecting' that, as a result of the search, they will find stolen or prohibited articles. Whether as the police officer you would have such reasonable grounds must be decided in the light of all the circumstances at the time. Usually it will be the behaviour of the person, perhaps combined with the location and time of day, or possibly information that you have received from a third party which will enable you to decide whether there are such reasonable grounds. As always you will have to be able to justify your decision after the event.

Once you have a reasonable suspicion then, and only then, can you stop someone in order to search them. It is not lawful for you to go on 'fishing expeditions' where you stop people with the intention of finding grounds to afford suspicion that they are carrying stolen or prohibited articles.

Reasonable suspicion can never be founded on the basis of purely personal factors such as a person's race, colour, age or hairstyle. The unacceptability of stereotyping people on the appearance or perceived membership of a particular group is discussed elsewhere in this book. Nevertheless, Code A does allow for the searching of members of gangs or groups who are known to habitually carry:

- knives unlawfully, or
- weapons, or
- controlled drugs

and who wear distinctive items of clothing or other things to identify themselves with such a group or gang.

12.4 **How?**

This is very important. Code A sets out how any search must be carried out. The cooperation of the person must be sought in every case and, although force could ultimately be used, this should be viewed very much as a last resort. Having stopped a person to search them, there is *no requirement* to do so. It may turn out from a moment's conversation that a search is either not required or it is impracticable to carry out.

An officer carrying out a search must provide their name and the police station to which they are attached to the person who is to be searched. If the officer is not in uniform they must also show the person their warrant card. They must also tell the person the purpose of the search and the grounds for it.

Generally when carrying out a search an officer cannot require the person to remove any clothing in public other than their outer coat, jacket and gloves. If for the purposes of the search it is necessary to go further than this (perhaps because the items being sought are very small, for example, stolen jewellery) then the person should be taken to a suitable private place, normally the nearest police station.

For each search and, generally speaking, at the time of the search, the officer must complete a search record. On the form are recorded the:

- name of the person searched, if they are willing to provide it—they are not obliged to—otherwise their description;
- date, time and location of the search;
- result of the search;
- grounds for the search.

The officer has to record there and then on the form the reasons why they stopped and searched the person. The subject of the search is entitled to a copy of the search record; this can be given at the time if they want it, or they can get a copy from the officer's station at a later date, up to a year after the search.

The ability to stop and search people is a valuable tool in tackling certain types of crime, however, it is a power which must be used properly and with great sensitivity and discretion.

12.5 **Powers of Entry**

If you enter someone else's property without their permission or some other legal authority you are a trespasser. This is a simple but important concept which we will come across later when we look at the offence of burglary. Although trespassing in this way is not generally a criminal offence, it does mean that the owner can ask you to leave—and throw you out by force if you don't go! This general rule applies as much to police officers as to anyone else. So if you want to go onto someone else's property you must either:

- be invited, or
- have a legal power of entry.

In some cases the owner of the property is assumed to have given general permission for restricted access to their property. Such general permission usually applies to people having lawful business at the house to walk up the path to the front door. Again such general permissions apply to police officers in the same way as everyone else. It is important to note that if someone goes beyond the limits of the permission, by walking round to the back door for instance, or roaming around the garden or failing to leave when asked, again they become trespassers.

The difficulty comes when not only does the owner not give permission, but actively wants to stop you from entering their property. In such cases if you do not have a legal power to go in then you cannot go in. Therefore, to enable the police to go into buildings to arrest people, to protect people, to search for things and to seize evidence, PACE, including Code B of the Codes of Practice, covers entry, search and seizure both with and without a warrant. Strangely enough, premises in this context also usually include boats, caravans and cars. As with other powers, these represent an interference with the private lives and property of individuals, and, therefore, must be used appropriately and only when necessary.

12.6 Powers Without Warrant

Police officers still retain a common law power of entry to prevent a breach of the peace (see Chapter 13). This power is only available when officers have a genuine and reasonable belief that a breach of the peace is happening or is about to happen in the immediate future; the sound of screaming and shouting and/or furniture and fittings being thrown around would be enough. PACE introduced wide powers of entry, search and seizure, particularly when made in connection with an arrest.

There are many Acts of Parliament that give the police (and other agencies) powers to apply to the courts for warrants authorising entry. There are also many other Acts which give the police powers of entry without a warrant. Examples of such powers are those that allow the police to enter:

- any place for the purpose of carrying out a search under the Firearms Act 1968;
- school premises in connection with weapons;
- relevant premises in connection with a police direction to leave and remove vehicles.

Of course, as we have seen, not everything a police officer does is related to crime and criminals. One occasion when an officer may need to get into a property quickly and without having to waste time seeking permission is when there is a fire inside. Section 17(1)(e) of PACE states that a constable may enter and search any premises for the purpose of saving life or preventing serious damage to property.

In this chapter we first saw that when a police officer reasonably suspects a person is carrying stolen or prohibited articles they may stop and detain them in order to search them for those articles. We then saw that the police do have some powers (mostly under PACE) to enter private property, regardless of the owner's consent. In order to be lawful these powers may only be used when they are necessary and proportionate to the task in hand.

This chapter and the previous one have been about the two most important police powers; in the next chapter we explore what a crime actually is.

FURTHER READING

→ <http://www.blackstonespolice.com>. Blackstone's are the main publishers of the standard police textbooks.

13

LAW AND ORDER

By any standards police duty is pretty unusual, if not unique. The motivation required to do it, along with the training and experience it gives you, and the level of personal responsibility it demands, makes policing very different from most other occupations. As well as the obvious commitment, energy and resilience, a sense of compassion and certainly humour, policing requires legal powers. We have already looked at some of those powers in the last two chapters.

Frequently, the role of the police in England and Wales is described as keeping law and order, but, as you have seen, the role is in fact much wider and far more complex than that. In this chapter we look at some of the key concepts in criminal law and then go on to consider some specific aspects of the law relevant to policing that are mainly concerned with keeping our communities safe.

13.1 The Law

For all officers, knowledge and use of the law is an essential skill. Not only is a great deal of time spent during initial training learning about the law and legal process, but this is constantly revisited as part of ongoing officer development. Certain specialist roles require enhanced legal knowledge in specific policing areas, such as fraud and public protection. Promotion exams are also heavily focused upon knowledge of the law. If, like most officers, this is your first detailed look at the law then it will probably seem very complicated and difficult to understand.

However, this is an area where knowledge really will empower your effectiveness as an operational officer and make the job a great deal more fulfilling, so where does law come from and what is it for? Well, put simply, law is essentially a set of rules necessary for the protection of the population and for good governance.

Most law is created from Acts of Parliament, also referred to as 'statute law', a process that involves proposals for a new law being subject to argument and scrutiny by politicians in both the House of Commons and House of Lords before finally being enacted. The Police and Criminal Evidence Act 1984 and the Theft Act 1968 are examples of laws that were passed through this process.

Common law is not written in any statute book and has been built up over many years by legal interpretations from court case decisions. Judges have a major part to play in this process, as their decisions can further define the legalities of police evidential processes and the way that prosecutions are approached.

Local councils can also apply to the Secretary of State for permission to operate bye laws covering particular activities, such as dog fouling. These are effectively local laws to deal with local problems and can be enforced like any other criminal offences and typically involve being given a fine.

Police officers are primarily concerned with the criminal law, which includes a wide range of offences explained more fully in Chapter 15. A simplistic overview of the criminal legal system is that persons summonsed or charged with criminal offences will appear before a court, which could be either, or both, a Magistrates' or Crown court. Prosecutions will be conducted by the Crown Prosecution Service (CPS), which comprises lawyers and legal executives specifically trained in prosecuting criminal cases and advising the police on legal matters.

13.2 It's a Crime

What actually is a crime? Well, the classification of some unlawful behaviour into 'crimes' is actually an administrative convenience. It is used by the Government, the police and other agencies to measure and monitor criminal activity.

Some criminal offences are clearly more serious than others. For instance, having the wrong sized letters on your car's number plate is a criminal offence (you can be punished in the Magistrates' court) and so is death by dangerous driving, but the two are totally different in terms of their consequences—both to the offender and the victim.

That doesn't mean that certain crimes are minor or trivial (if you want to know what crimes are 'minor' ask the victim—the answer will almost certainly be 'none'). However, the law has to treat some criminal offences as being of more significance than others. As a result some offences carry a greater maximum penalty than others. For these reasons the law divides criminal offences into 'summary offences' and 'indictable offences'.

13.3 Summary Offences

Summary offences include almost all road traffic offences such as speeding and careless driving. However, just because an offence is classified as summary that does not mean that it is less than significant. The list of summary offences includes some offences relating to public disorder and anti-social behaviour, drunkenness and taking a vehicle without the owner's consent. These are common offences that can frequently have a significant impact on the quality of people's lives, and some are in themselves substantial offences that can attract prison sentences.

Summary offences have to be tried in the Magistrates' court, either by a district judge (a qualified and experienced lawyer) or by a bench of lay magistrates—people from the local community appointed as justices of the peace. Both lay magistrates and district judges have the power to fine those found guilty or, where the offence allows, send them to prison for up to six months. The overwhelming majority of criminal cases (about 95 per cent according to recent figures) are dealt with in the Magistrates' courts.

13.4 **Indictable Offences**

Indictable offences are those which have more serious consequences for the victims and the community, not to mention any person that is found guilty of them. Examples would be rape, robbery, the more serious assaults, some burglaries and, of course, murder. They are called indictable because they are tried on indictment, that is to say in the Crown court before a judge and, in most cases, a jury.

The judge in the Crown court will be an experienced lawyer with many years' experience of criminal practice. He or she is there to preside over the trial and to decide on matters of law (such as whether a defence applied in a particular case) and on some matters of fact. The jury is made up of 12 members of the community chosen, as far as practicable, by chance. Their job is to decide on questions of fact—such as whether the defendant is guilty! Generally speaking, individual jurors only ever sit on one case in their entire lives.

If, having heard all the evidence that the judge allows, the jury decides that the defendant is guilty, the judge will pass sentence. Though there are guidelines, judges have very wide discretion when it comes to punishment. The fact that an offence carries a maximum prison sentence of many years (theft for example has a maximum penalty of seven years' imprisonment) does not mean that the guilty party will receive anything like that amount or even be sent to prison at all. The only exception to this is the offence of murder where a life sentence is mandatory, though even then the judge has to apply some discretion in deciding how long the person must serve before being considered for parole. Incidentally, when it comes to the investigation of crime, police officers have additional powers available to them when enquiring into indictable offences.

13.5 **Either-Way Offences**

The fact that criminal offences are divided into summary and indictable does not mean that every offence falls into one or other of those categories;

114

very little in English and Welsh law is that straightforward. There is in fact a third category; offences that can be tried in either the Magistrates' court or the Crown court—the choice is usually the defendant's (though the magistrates can refuse to hear it if they think their powers of sentence insufficient for the circumstances of the crime in question). Such offences are known as 'either-way offences'. These include theft, handling stolen goods, criminal deceptions, some assaults and drug offences.

13.6 **Order**

Think back to Part I and you may remember that the prime duty of the police is to keep the peace and protect life and property. This has remained unchanged since the first 'modern' police force was formed in 1829.

The police have a number of legal powers to help them maintain order. The oldest of these comes from the idea of a 'breach of the peace'. Generally speaking a breach of the peace occurs when a person is harmed, or they or their property is threatened by some form of disturbance. In such situations the police have the power to enter premises and to detain anyone who is causing the disturbance or threatening the person or property. As discussed above, these powers come from the decisions of judges over the centuries known as the 'common law' and not from any Act of Parliament. Breach of the peace is not an offence and you cannot be charged with it; it is a complaint on behalf of the community for which you can be detained until it is no longer likely or brought before a court and bound over to be of good behaviour.

Whilst the powers to deal with a breach of the peace are important (and in practical terms the power to enter premises is a very valuable one), they are seldom used these days; the problem being that you can only detain a person as long as is necessary to prevent the breach of the peace. In practice the person has almost certainly committed a substantive offence for which they can be arrested, provided the necessity test has been met and, most certainly, can be prosecuted. These criminal

115

offences range from simply being drunk in a public place through to harassment, causing an affray, and finally rioting; to say nothing of any actual assault that may have taken place.

Whilst the police may have extensive powers to deal with individual cases of public disorder, it has now been recognised that the job of keeping the peace, preventing crime and disorder and ensuring quality of life in the community cannot be left to the police alone. The task is both too big and too complex. That is why we now have initiatives like the Community Crime and Disorder Reduction Partnerships, as discussed in Chapter 6.

What follows in the next two chapters is an introduction to some key principles of the criminal law and a brief examination of some of the more common offences you will be expected to deal with on a day-to-day basis. It will give you a taste for the type of knowledge you will need to gain and it will help to build the foundations for any further training you undertake.

FURTHER READING

→ Rebecca Huxley-Binns, *Unlocking the English Legal System*, 2005, Hodder Arnold.

→ Johnston & Hutton, *Blackstone's Police Manual Evidence & Procedure*, 2011.

14

A QUICK LESSON IN CRIME

We have hinted at this elsewhere but it is worth stating again here formally because it is so important. There are two main reasons why, as a police officer, you need to know the detail of all common criminal offences:

- because you need to know what you will need to prove;
- because you need to recognise if an offence has been committed, and if so what type, so you know what powers are available to you.

A police officer who doesn't know the intricacies of at least the every-day offences is like a carpenter who does not know how to use a plane—ineffective.

Even though every criminal offence is, like a recipe, made up of its own particular ingredients (such as theft, whose ingredients include dishonesty, the taking of someone else's property and the intention to permanently deprive the owner of it), there are some basic principles that apply in nearly all circumstances. Let's look at those first.

14.1 Guilty Knowledge

There is a rule in the criminal law that actions alone cannot amount to a crime; they have to be accompanied by an intention to do wrong—or at least a realisation that their actions are wrong. This intention is known as the 'guilty mind' or 'guilty knowledge'. The Latin term that is sometimes still used is '*mens rea*'.

There are some offences where a guilty mind is not required, generally road traffic offences, such as speeding. These are known as absolute offences. However, as a general rule you can assume that only if someone had the intention to do wrong when they carried out their actions can they be liable for 'committing a crime'. An example of this principle in action would be if, while you were out shopping today, your mind was on other things (like a new career in the police), and you wandered out of the shop without paying for the goods you were holding, you would not have stolen them. Your actions in leaving the shop without paying would not be enough to make you guilty of theft, because you had no wrongful intention—no guilty mind. This rule protects people who may have some mental impairment or who are not capable of understanding the consequences of their actions. It also protects people whose innocent actions go wrong—or just those who go through life in a daydream.

One common situation where people may not know what they are doing is when they are drunk. So does this mean that drunkenness amounts to 'blameless behaviour'? The answer is, 'No'—if not knowing what you were doing because you were drunk gave you a general 'get out of jail free' card, how many people would ever be convicted of anything, especially crimes involving public order and violence?

There are special rules for drunkenness—generally you cannot avoid conviction for most crimes simply by showing you were too drunk or too 'high' on drugs to know what you were doing, but, as always, there are some exceptions.

For some offences it is not necessary to show that the person intended to do wrong, merely that they were reckless as to whether their actions would do harm. There are many different mental states that meet the requirements of different offences. However, as a general rule some degree of 'guilty mind' is needed.

14.2 **Wrongful Acts**

The other key element that is needed is the 'wrongful act'. This may sound obvious but it isn't always. Simply having a guilty mind or intention to do wrong can never, on its own, amount to a crime. If bad thoughts were a crime we would all be in a lot of trouble. To prove that a person committed a crime you have to prove that they did the relevant wrongful act as well. Using our example of the theft again, we would need to show that they actually took the property.

The other thing you need to note about the 'wrongful act' is that you have to show that the person did the act voluntarily, that they were in control of their movements at the time. For example, if you had a sneezing fit whilst driving your car and, as a result, crashed into another car, you could not be held responsible for driving badly.

There are a few offences where, rather than having to prove the person did something they should not have, you will need to prove they did not do something that they should have done. There are not many of these offences because generally the law is about stopping people doing bad things not forcing them to do good. However, there are a few occasions where a person will commit a crime by failing to act. These are usually where a person has a legal duty or a special relationship towards another person. Examples here would be parents neglecting their children, or a police officer who fails to at least try to prevent an assault.

14.3 **Unfinished Offences**

Staying with the idea of criminal acts, there are a special group of crimes—'incomplete' or unfinished offences. These are offences where, for one reason or another, the person committing them doesn't manage to achieve what they have set out to do. However, such an action, or attempt, is a criminal offence even though it was not successful, and the law treats any person guilty of an attempted crime in exactly the same way as if the offence had been completed. They are also liable to exactly the same punishment.

14.4 **Defences**

When considering criminal offences, it is important to think of what *defences* the accused person might have. Some serious crimes have specific defences written into them, while all have some possible form of defence. As a police officer you need to know about the defences just as much as the points to prove. Why? Well there are two main reasons:

- because the police have a duty to investigate crimes fairly and impartially—if there is evidence that supports a person's defence then you need to collect it just as diligently as evidence that points to his or her guilt;
- because if you don't know what the defences are you will not be able to deal with them when you come to interview the accused person.

14.5 **Proof**

'Proof' is a little word with big consequences. Remember that a person can only be convicted of a criminal offence if there is proof of each and every ingredient of that offence. Criminal trials in England and Wales are not about what actually happened—they are about whether the prosecution can prove the guilt of the accused.

There are only three ways of proving a person's involvement in a criminal offence:

- witnesses;
- admission by the individual; and
- forensic evidence.

And the greatest of the three is forensic evidence. Witnesses can be forgetful, mistaken, dishonest or just unreliable, especially when it comes to identification evidence. Additionally jurors sometimes disbelieve them for no other reason than their appearance. Admissions are more reliable than they used to be now that solicitors sit in on almost every interview, but they cannot always be obtained and they can always be withdrawn. Forensic evidence, however, is hard and tangible, the jury can see it and it is very difficult for the defence to attack solid physical evidence—provided it has been properly and lawfully collected and presented. The ideal, of course, is to have all three types of evidence, all saying the same thing, but that seldom happens.

As pointed out above it is not the job of the police simply to collect evidence against the accused person. They must collect all the evidence relating to the crime, impartially and efficiently, and present it to the Crown Prosecution Service (CPS). It is the CPS that will make the decision whether or not to take the person before the courts and will manage the entire process.

In gathering and presenting evidence there are two key rules to remember.

The first rule

The defendant does not have to prove that they did not commit the offence; it is the prosecution's job to prove that they did. Everyone is innocent unless and until they are proved guilty. A famous judge once described this as being the 'golden thread' that ran throughout the criminal justice system.

The second rule

The prosecution must present enough evidence and sufficiently strong evidence to prove the defendant's guilt beyond reasonable doubt. It is not enough to be able to show that it is likely that the defendant committed the offence or even that it is probable that they did so.

The court will not convict unless they are *sure*—beyond reasonable doubt—that the defendant is guilty.

14.6 **Remember the Victim**

For every crime there is at least one victim. Crime does not just happen; it involves real people suffering real loss and real harm. Even in what are wrongly called 'victimless' crimes (such as the possession of drugs and offences relating to prostitution) people are still being hurt—often the offenders themselves, and certainly the well-being of the community at large is damaged.

Certain victims are especially vulnerable, such as those who are too old, too young or otherwise unable to look after themselves. People who have been the victim of crimes on more than one occasion are known as 'repeat victims', also fall into the category of vulnerable victims.

Crime can be a fascinating subject and studying it will throw up all sorts of scenarios and variations. Investigating it is even more engrossing. Whether studying or investigating, it is very easy to become detached and clinical. So you need always to remember the victim and be sympathetic to their needs.

Now that you know what a crime is and the basics of proof, in the next chapter we will look at the common offences that, as a police officer, you will have to deal with.

FURTHER READING

→ Christopher Allen, *Practical Guide to Evidence,* 2004, Cavendish Publishing Ltd.

15

LAW AND ORDER: A CLOSER LOOK

Having now briefly examined the principles that underpin the criminal law, it is time to look at some specific offences in more detail. The ones we will look at are those which as a uniformed officer you can expect to have to deal with on a regular basis and some of them almost every day.

15.1 **Offences Against Property**

The majority of all crimes committed in England and Wales involve property in some way; as a police officer they will make up the majority of your case-load. Indeed, the offence of 'theft' accounts for around half of all recorded crime on its own.

Property crime not only covers the stealing of other people's property; it also includes damaging and destroying property, breaking into homes, business premises and schools, and taking vehicles without the owner's consent before subsequently abandoning them. Property crime is the cause of a great deal of misery and distress to the victims. Not only does it bring unhappiness and expense to the people whose property has been stolen or damaged, property crime also:

- has an enormous impact on the economy (every price in every major shop is a little higher than it otherwise would be and every credit card charges a little extra interest to cover the costs of fraud);
- creates fear of crime in many communities and so damages the quality of life for everyone;
- uses up a considerable amount of police time and resources.

Some property crimes—such as burglary—can include injury or harm to the occupier of the property as well. As a result of all of the above, most property crimes carry substantial prison sentences. So let's look at some of the main property crimes.

Theft

You may think that you have a fair idea of what is involved in an offence of theft. So why not take a couple of minutes, before reading on, to note down what you think the ingredients are?

In police training, offences are given as 'definitions' which include the 'points to prove' (the ingredients). They are not normally just a copy of the section from the Act of Parliament; instead they use phrases in standard English so that they become more meaningful and easier to remember. Many forces insist that all new recruits learn the definitions of key offences and also those that relate to the most used police powers.

A person is guilty of theft if they:

> Dishonestly appropriate property belonging to another with the intention of permanently depriving the other of it.
> Thief and steal shall be construed accordingly.
> Section 1 of the Theft Act 1968, maximum penalty on indictment 7 years, triable either way.

There in a nutshell you have the offence of theft. Of course learning definitions by heart is not much use unless you know what they mean, so let's look at the points to prove.

Dishonestly

'Dishonestly' means that the person behaved in a way that would be seen by the average citizen as dishonest. Section 2 of the Act sets out three sets of circumstances in which the person's action would not be regarded as dishonest—remember we spoke in the previous chapter about defences.

Appropriates

Most thefts involve someone simply taking something. However, there are circumstances where a person dishonestly gets ownership of someone else's property without actually 'taking' it. Consequently in section 3 of the Act, 'appropriates' is defined to mean assuming the rights of ownership.

Property

It seems obvious that you can only commit theft if you actually take something. The problem comes when we look at what that 'something' could be. How about the balance in your bank account? That doesn't actually exist as a physical thing—it's only a record in a computer database, but you would be rather upset if someone took it away from you. How would you feel if, whilst out walking, you picked some mushrooms that were growing wild in a field intending to cook them for your dinner and you were promptly arrested for theft? You can see how complex the idea of property is when it comes to theft. Consequently, we will just note that a bank balance can be stolen but mushrooms growing wild cannot (unless you do it for gain or reward) and, for now, leave it at that.

Belonging to another

Again it probably seems obvious that you cannot steal your own property. Well, actually in law there are certain circumstances where you can, but you can ignore these for now. Generally speaking you need to prove that the property belonged to someone other than the person appropriating it and that they knew this to be the case.

Intention to permanently deprive

This is essential and sometimes it can be the hardest part to prove. If someone takes something belonging to someone else but intends to give it back, whole and complete, and at a later date, then they will not have committed theft. For this reason there is a specific offence which deals with taking a vehicle without permission and later abandoning it, which we will look at in a moment.

At this point, how did your 'layperson's' view of what theft was about compare to the real thing? Probably, if you were like most people, you had the sense of it but not the detail.

If evidence to prove any one of the above points is missing then you have not got an offence of theft (or at least not one you can prove).

EXAMPLE

Petra, a college student, runs out of milk and doesn't have the money, at the moment, to buy any more. She sees some bottles of milk on the doorstep of the house opposite. So she takes a bottle of milk intending to use it with her breakfast but also to replace it with some other milk later that day. Someone sees her and calls the police. If you were the police officer what would you do?

You know what the points to prove are for an offence of theft, so let's look at each in turn. The first problem is to decide whether Petra was dishonest. If she knows the neighbours well enough, it might have been that she thought they would have given her permission to take the milk had she asked them, and in law this might well provide her with a defence. On the other hand, perhaps she knows them well enough to know they would have refused, which might be why she did not ask. So we can note that this is an area that we will have to explore in interview. We certainly can't prove this point yet, but we do have enough to afford sufficient suspicion that we can carry on. The next point is, has she 'appropriated' the milk? Yes she has; she walked across the road and took it. The fact that it belonged to another is also straightforward. The final point is the intention to permanently deprive, can we prove this? Well, yes we can, depending on what she has done with the milk by the time we arrive. We may need to clarify the point in interview, but her intention was to use the milk with her breakfast. That would mean that she had permanently deprived the owner of it. The fact that she intended to replace the milk with another bottle is irrelevant; even if she did so it would not have been the same milk. So we have sufficient evidence to afford reasonable grounds to suspect Petra is guilty of theft and, depending what she says in interview on the subject of dishonesty, the case is capable of being proved.

Robbery

Now that you understand theft, you are most of the way to understanding robbery. People sometimes use the term 'robbing' in relation to shops, cars, and buildings. They may say something like, 'I have had my car robbed' or 'They robbed her house last week'. In fact, and in law, only people can be robbed. Robbery is simply a theft which is accompanied by violence or the threat of violence to a person. If there is no theft there is no robbery—though there may be an attempt (remember 'unfinished offences' from the last chapter) or an offence of assault. Robbery can range from an incident in which a mobile phone is snatched and force or threats of force are used towards the owner, to an armed hold-up of a bank or security van.

The key additional ingredient is that the use of force, or the threat to use immediate force, must precede the theft and be used or threatened in order that the theft can take place. It is not necessary that the force be used or offered to the owner of the property but it must be against a person who is actually present. There is no need for a weapon to be used, nor is there an offence of armed robbery or robbery with violence (though the presence of any of these three things will affect the sentence handed down by the court). Robbery is a very serious offence and can only be tried in the crown court.

Burglary

Just as only people can be robbed, only *buildings* can be burgled. Burglary is a more complicated offence than theft or robbery. However, there are some key features that, once you understand them, will make everything clear.

First there are two types of burglary: one deals with the offender's intentions at the time they enter the building, whilst the other deals with the burglar's actions once inside the building. Grasp this and it is pretty well straightforward.

Type 1: Intentions

The ingredients of the first type of burglary are:

- entering a building (or a part of a building)—this can include reaching through an open window or leaning through a door;
- as a trespasser—we looked at what this meant back in Chapter 12 so we don't need to repeat it here. Note that it is possible to enter premises with full permission but either go into a part of the building where you don't have permission, or remain concealed until after your permission has expired—in both cases one can become a trespasser even though the original entry was lawful;
- intending to do one or more of three other crimes, i.e.—
  - steal
  - inflict serious injury on anyone inside
  - cause damage to the property or anything in it.

Note that this is a crime of *intention*, the burglar does not have to carry out any theft, etc.—it is enough that he or she intended to do so at the time they entered the building, or part of a building, as a trespasser. You might want to think about how you could prove to a court that a person had the required intention—look back at the section on proof in the last chapter and refresh your memory of the three types of evidence and think about how you could, perhaps, use each to prove the point. Of course if the burglar actually goes on to carry out one of the three offences that would be pretty good supporting evidence of their intention at the time of entry. If they do go on to steal or inflict serious injury on someone inside the building, then they commit the second type of burglary.

Type 2: Behaviour after entering

The second type of burglary is concerned with what the offender does after entering the building or part of a building as a trespasser. If they steal anything (or try to) or inflict serious injury on anyone inside the building (or try to), they commit this offence. There is no requirement to have to prove any intention on behalf of the offender.

You can see that there is a big overlap between the two types of burglary and often both will have been committed in the same set of circumstances. Another example may be needed.

EXAMPLE

A man who has gone into a pub for a drink with friends visits the toilets. He hides in the toilets until the pub has closed, when he goes back into the bar room and takes a bottle of whiskey and some cigarettes from behind the bar. The landlord hears a noise from the bar and calls the police. What offence do you think might have been committed and why?

The starting point in deciding whether the man has committed either type of burglary is whether or not he was a trespasser. At the time the man went into the toilets he was a customer of the pub and had permission to be there—like all the people using the pub—so he wasn't then trespassing. However, once the pub closed, the man no longer had the permission and he now became a trespasser. Once he re-enters the bar area the first part of the offence is complete; he has entered a part of a building as a trespasser. The question to be answered now is what his intention was at that time. If he intended to steal the cigarettes and whiskey then he was guilty of the first type of burglary. When he takes the goods from behind the bar he dishonestly appropriates property belonging to the landlord, intending to permanently deprive him of it. We know this is theft and so the man is guilty, at this point in time, of the second type of burglary.

Burglary is a serious offence that can have considerable impact on the victims—especially if the building involved is their home. It is worth remembering what was said earlier about the victims of crime. The effect of burglary on people's feeling of security, and that of their families, can be devastating. The burglary of homes (known in police parlance as 'burglary dwelling') is treated by the courts as a particularly serious crime.

Taking vehicles

We saw earlier that if the offender dishonestly takes someone else's property but has no intention of permanently depriving the owner of it the offence of theft has not been committed. So if someone without your permission takes your mobile phone, perhaps for a prank, and then, without using it, leaves it in the next office, they have not committed any offence. However, if someone takes your car without your permission and leaves it in the next street then they have committed an offence under section 12 of the Theft Act 1968, taking a motor vehicle or other conveyance without authority.

This offence is known by many names in different parts of the country and across different police forces: 'unlawful taking of a motor vehicle (UTMV)', 'taking and driving away (TDA)' and 'taking without consent (TWOC)' are probably the most common variations. Another name commonly used in some newspapers is 'joy riding'. There is nothing joyous about this offence. It creates fear, frustration and expense to the owner and the community—not to mention the large numbers of people every year who are killed and injured by criminals driving cars that they have taken without the consent of the owner. There is a further, aggravated, form of this offence that occurs when the vehicle is used in certain incidents before the owner gets it back. This carries a longer sentence than the six months that the 'basic' offence can attract.

The offence of taking vehicles does have a statutory defence. If the person who took the vehicle believed that:

- they had a lawful authority to use the vehicle, or
- the owner would have consented had they known of the taking *and* the circumstances of it.

To see what this second defence could mean in practice let's look at another example.

EXAMPLE

A student living in a hall of residence usually allows a fellow resident to use her motor bike to go to the gym every Tuesday and Thursday. One Tuesday our student could not be found by her fellow resident and so he took the bike anyway. After all, he thought, he only wanted to go to the gym as usual and the owner had always let him use the bike for that. The owner comes back and finds that the bike is missing. She calls the police for advice and you take the call. What would you tell her?

First, has the fellow student taken the motor bike? The answer is 'Yes'. Next, did he have the owner's consent? Well, not specifically; however, he believed that if he had asked her if he could borrow the bike to go to the gym she would have said yes because he had regularly been given permission to do so in the past. For this reason he has a full defence and does not commit the offence. If he had taken the bike to go on an amateur motor-cross rally, then it would have been a different matter entirely.

As a final note, it is also an offence to take a lift from someone when you know they have taken the conveyance without the owner's consent.

Going equipped

Imagine that you are a police officer on patrol late one evening in an area where there have been a lot of burglaries, when a member of the public points out a man to you and says he saw him behaving suspiciously near the side door of a locked shop. He further says that when the man saw him he seemed to put something inside his coat and walk away quite quickly. You quite rightly stop and search the man and find in an inside pocket a tyre lever and some thin rubber gloves. What can you do about it? Well, these are precisely the sort of circumstances that the offence of 'going equipped' was designed to deal with.

Under section 25 of the Theft Act 1968 it is an offence for any person, when not at their home address, to have in their possession any article for use in connection with or in the course of any burglary or theft. 'Articles' here mean anything that the person intended to use in the commission of one of either of the two types of offence. Examples would be screwdrivers, knives, gloves or disguises. So in our example the evidence provided by the member of the public together with the spate of burglaries in the area would be sufficient to prove that the man had possession at that time of the tyre lever and gloves intending to use them in connection with a burglary.

Proving intention, as we have seen, can be tricky. So you will be pleased to hear that if the article was made or adapted for use in the commission of one of the offences, then that is sufficient proof—there is no need to worry about the intention of the suspect.

'Going equipped' is a very useful tool for officers and what is even better is it enables you to deal with criminals *before* they have committed a crime which harms a victim.

Criminal damage

The main law containing the relevant offences is the Criminal Damage Act 1971. Section 1 makes it an offence to deliberately or recklessly damage someone else's property unless you have a lawful excuse. An example of a lawful excuse would be a police officer who damages a door whilst making correct use of one of their powers to enter a building.

That it is an offence to damage someone else's property is probably to be expected. However, it is also an offence to damage your own property in circumstances where, deliberately or recklessly, someone else's life would be endangered. Perhaps an example would be someone who chopped down a large tree in their garden in such a manner that caused it to fall into a busy road. Even if nobody was hurt, such an act would constitute an offence under the Criminal Damage Act. Criminal damage offences where fire is used are known as arson.

The Act also makes it an offence to threaten to damage or destroy property and to have in your possession articles to be used for damaging or destroying property. So a threat to smash up someone's home or car is an offence in itself, as is having a tin of aerosol paint with which to spray graffiti.

'Aggravated damage' happens when the offender damages property and intends to endanger someone's life or is reckless as to whether life would be endangered. An example of this very serious offence would be throwing a brick through the windscreen of a moving car. Aggravated damage offences often involve the use of fire (examples of people putting petrol through someone's letter box followed by a lighted match appear all too often in the press) and this is the most serious form of criminal damage—it carries a maximum penalty of life imprisonment.

Racially or religiously aggravated offences

For many years there has been particular concern at the additional evil of crimes that were specifically aimed at racial groups or which were motivated by hostility towards a person's racial origin. The Crime and Disorder Act 1998 revisited the issue of racially aggravated crime. The result was the identification of a number of offences that would be treated as being far more serious by the police and the courts if they are shown to be racially aggravated. This was subsequently extended to include religiously aggravated offences.

Generally an offence will be deemed to be racially or religiously aggravated if:

- at the time of committing it (or immediately before/after), the offender demonstrated towards the victim hostility based on the victim's membership of a racial or religious group; or
- the offence was motivated by hostility towards members of a racial or religious group based on their membership of that group.

Criminal damage is an offence that can be racially or religiously aggravated. The other offences include assaults and some offences relating to public disorder.

15.2 Offences Against People

The next group of offences to consider relates to those committed directly against people. Generally these are categorised according to the amount of injury that the assailant caused or intended to cause to their victim. At the lowest end of the scale we have common assault, where no lasting injury is done, and at the top we have manslaughter and murder—though a detailed examination of these last two are outside the scope of this book.

Generally speaking, offences against people involve assaults (and also what is technically known as battery—the actual application of physical force). If unlawful force (or a real threat of it) is used towards another person an offence will have been committed. The next step is to decide which one and, as we have said, this is determined by the amount of injury caused.

If no lasting injury is caused—nothing much more than, perhaps, a temporary reddening of the skin—then it will be a common assault. You should note that the normal accidental knocking against or unintended jostling against other people will not amount to an assault. There has to be a deliberate use of force. If the injury is a little more serious, say a black eye or a minor cut, then it would be an offence of 'assault occasioning actual bodily harm' under section 47 of the Offences Against the Person Act 1861. If the injury involves a serious cut or a broken bone or other serious harm, you would be looking at an offence of 'causing grievous bodily harm or wounding' under section 20 of the 1861 Act, unless the assailant intended to cause such a level of injury, in which case it would be an offence under section 18 and regarded by the courts as much more serious (it carries a maximum penalty of life imprisonment). All three levels of assault can be racially or religiously motivated.

15.3 **Offences Against the Peace**

In this section we will take a look at those offences relating to the disturbance of people's peaceful enjoyment of their private, public or community life.

Our starting point is the breach of the peace. This is not an offence as such, though as we saw in Chapter 12 you can be detained if you are committing one and it does provide a very handy power of entry for the astute officer. However, as was mentioned, if a person is committing a breach of the peace, particularly in a public place, they are probably committing a substantial offence and it is almost always better to use that to deal with the person and the situation. So let's look at the substantial offences that may be open to us.

The Act that we are concerned with here is the Public Order Act 1986. As with assaults this Act provides a number of offences of increasing severity.

Section 5—Harassment, alarm and distress

This offence is committed when a person:

- uses threatening, abusive or insulting words or behaviour, or disorderly behaviour, or

135

- displays any writing, sign or other visible representation which is threatening, abusive or insulting, within the hearing or sight of a person likely to be caused harassment, alarm or distress thereby.

This offence is used in cases which amount to less serious incidents of anti-social behaviour. Where violence has been used, unless it was of a very minor nature, it is not normally appropriate. There must be a person within the sight or hearing of the offender who is likely to be caused harassment, alarm or distress by the conduct in question. Although in strict theory this could be a police officer, in practice you will not get a conviction if the only people that were likely to be harassed etc. were the police. Additionally you need to be aware that although you need to prove that there was such a person who was likely to have been caused harassment, alarm or distress, there is no requirement for them to actually provide evidence to that effect. Your own observations of the reactions of members of the public to the incident will usually be enough. This offence can be racially and religiously aggravated.

Section 4a—Intentional harassment, alarm or distress

This offence was added in as an afterthought by the Criminal Justice and Public Order Act 1994. It is the next one up the scale from section 5 and its provisions are identical except that under this offence you have to prove that the language or behaviour was used or the sign was displayed with the *intention* of causing harassment, alarm or distress. This offence can be racially and religiously aggravated.

Section 4—Fear or provocation of violence

This offence is regarded as equal in severity to section 4a and this time the person using the insulting words and behaviour, etc. must do so with *intent* to cause a person to believe that immediate unlawful violence will be used or with the intent to provoke another into the immediate use of unlawful violence. This offence can be racially and religiously aggravated.

Section 3—Affray

The offence of affray occurs where a person uses or threatens unlawful violence towards another and this conduct would cause a person of reasonable firmness present at the scene to fear for his or her personal safety. The seriousness of this offence lies in the effect the conduct of the offender has on persons other than the person towards whom he or she is directing his or her violence. Some third party, uninvolved in the violence, must be put in fear for this offence to be complete. The Crown Prosecution Service advises that suitable circumstances for charging an offence of affray would include:

> A fight between two or more people in a place where members of the general public are present (for example in a public house, discotheque, restaurant or street) with a level of violence such as would put them in substantial fear (as opposed to passing concern) for their safety (even though the fighting is not directed towards them).

Section 2—Violent disorder

Violent disorder is very similar to affray except that there must be at least three people who are acting together in a concerted act of violence. When there is serious public disorder at a public event (such as a football match) and violence is used towards the police this may well be a suitable charge for those arrested.

Section 1—Riot

Conduct which falls under the offence of riot is thankfully very rare. It requires that at least 12 people be acting together and using violence for a common purpose and that the conduct of them taken together was such that it did cause a person of reasonable firmness present at the scene to fear for his or her personal safety. The Crown Prosecution Service will normally only proceed with a charge of riot in the most serious cases usually linked to planned or spontaneous serious outbreaks of sustained violence.

Offensive and anti-social behaviour

Aside from the substantive offences we have looked at, another measure to deal with offensive and anti-social behaviour that is open to the police is the 'anti-social behaviour order' more commonly known by its initials 'ASBO'. An ASBO is an order made by a civil court that requires the named person to refrain from specific behaviour, associating with named individuals or going to a specified area. It lasts for a minimum period of two years, and can be served on anyone over 10 years old. The intention of the order is to protect the public from further harm rather than to punish the offender, so the issuing of an ASBO does not count as a criminal conviction. Neither is it necessary that the person has been convicted of any offence—though in practice the court will require evidence of persistent anti-social behaviour before making an order and what better evidence than a string of relevant convictions. If the person breaches their order they then commit a criminal offence for which they can be arrested and punished.

Drunkenness

Any experienced police officer will tell you that most of the violence and anti-social behaviour that occurs on the streets is fuelled by alcohol, and this has been borne out by official studies. Therefore, it should be no surprise that the police have powers relating to drink.

There is a particular offence of being drunk and disorderly and all that needs to be proved is that the person was behaving in a disorderly way whilst drunk in a public place. Interestingly, when it comes to proof that a person was in fact drunk, the word of a constable is deemed sufficient.

The police also have a power under the Confiscation of Alcohol (Young Persons) Act 1997. In brief this says that, where a constable reasonably suspects that a person in a public place is in possession of alcohol and that:

- the person is under the age of 18, or

- the person intends that the drink should be drunk by a person under the age of 18, or
- a person under the age of 18 who is with that person has recently consumed alcohol,

the constable may require the person to surrender anything that is in their possession that the constable reasonably believes to be alcohol and to state their name and address.

There are further offences and powers that allow the police to deal with drunkenness and street drinking in areas that have been specially designated by the local authority. You may have seen notices specifying such places. More senior police officers have additional powers to order premises to be closed where there is anti-social behaviour involving the sale of alcohol.

15.4 Offences Against Policy

Some criminal offences are not committed against any particular person or property, though, as we have already discussed, such crimes still have victims. For the purposes of this book we will categorise these crimes as 'offences against policy', because the fact that the behaviour is illegal has been decided by the policies of the Government of the day and include certain sexual acts where all the parties are consenting, to the possession of weapons and drugs.

Controlled drugs

The use of controlled drugs is the root cause of a great deal of crime. A recent study revealed that no fewer than 80 per cent of the prisoners in a prison were drug users or had been sentenced for a drug-related crime, and fully 40 per cent of all women in prison have been sentenced for drug offences (possession, importation or trafficking). It is also notable that a large proportion of thefts (particularly shoplifting) and burglaries are committed by people who are trying to obtain money to buy drugs. Furthermore, the criminal gangs seeking to protect the area in which they have a monopoly on the drug trade from other gangs frequently resort to extreme violence, including murder.

Not that long ago drugs were a problem only in some areas of larger cities; they are now available in every town and large village in the country, and the crime and social problems have spread accordingly. As a police officer this is an area of the law you will quickly be involved in.

Controlled drugs are divided into three categories or classes: A, B and C, although officers need only concern themselves with the first two classes. The decision about which class a substance should belong to depends on its effect on the individual using it. Class A drugs are the most dangerous and include heroin, cocaine, LSD and ecstasy; in Class B are barbiturates and cannabis. The category of a particular drug determines the maximum sentence that can be handed down by the courts.

There are three main drug offences that you will be involved in:

- simple possession—where the drug is intended for personal use or no other purpose can be proved;
- possession with intent to supply the drug to someone else;
- supplying or offering to supply someone else with a controlled drug.

There are other offences involving the production and importation of controlled drugs, but as a uniformed officer you are not likely to have to deal with these and so they are outside the scope of this book.

In practical terms if you find someone in possession of a quantity of, say, white powder you will not know if it is heroin or washing powder. Therefore, most arrests for drug offences are made on the basis of reasonable suspicion and charges are only made after the substance has been analysed.

Weapons

The carrying of weapons has become an issue of considerable concern over recent years. In particular, the use of knives in crime has caused some notable changes in the law. For these reasons, the powers to stop and search people that we discussed in Chapter 12 were made available to the police in relation to weapons.

Generally the law makes a distinction between knives and similar articles and other sorts of weapon. Firearms are a particular group of weapons that attract very strict controls and these are outside the scope of this book, though, as a rule, it will be an offence for most people to have handguns, rifles, shotguns or ammunition for any of them unless they have specific authority to do so.

Although you may be familiar with terms such as 'offensive weapon', the law in this area is wide and complex, going far beyond making it an offence to have such items. Some legislation is aimed at preventing people carrying certain weapons, while in other areas it is concerned with the sale or use of weapons. For now all you need to know is that it is an offence for a person to have an offensive weapon with them in a public place without lawful authority or reasonable excuse.

What is an offensive weapon? Well, it is defined as being something that has been made or adapted or is intended for causing injury to someone else. An example of something made for causing injury would be a bayonet. As with the offence of going equipped, unless the article has been made or adapted for causing injury you are going to have to prove intention.

EXAMPLE

Police officers carrying batons whilst on duty, or members of the armed forces carrying bayonets on parade, have offensive weapons with them in a public place. However, they have 'lawful authority'. Similarly, people having the tools of their trade with them in the course of their work (for example, Stanley knives for fitting carpets) would probably have a 'reasonable excuse'—as long as they didn't carry them intending to use them for causing injury.

There is also an offence of carrying a knife or other bladed or sharply pointed instrument in a public place (or on school premises) without good reason or lawful authority. For this offence there is no requirement that the person had the item with them for a particular purpose; mere possession in public is enough. There is, though, an exception for small pen-knives provided the cutting edge of the blade is not longer than 3 inches (7.72 cm).

As mentioned previously, there are other offences aimed at restricting the supply of weapons and their availability in England and Wales. In particular there is a specific offence relating to the sale of knives to people under the age of 16.

In this chapter you have learned some of the basics about the most common offences a street-duty officer has to deal with. This will have given you a flavour for the extent of knowledge the ordinary constable has to have to do their job properly and if you do join the Service, you will have a flying start in the theoretical aspect of your initial training.

FURTHER READING

➡ <http://www.blackstonespolice.com>. Blackstone's are the main publishers of the standard police textbooks.

Appendix 1

GLOSSARY OF POLICE TERMS

Like many jobs the police service has its own informal language; you will learn a whole new vocabulary when you join. Within this vocabulary, many short-hand expressions have developed in the police setting. Nicknames, letters and abbreviations—even numbers—the police language can be very confusing when it is first encountered. Although the list below contains some of the more common references used in the police, some expressions differ from one force to another.

Organisations and Agencies

ACPO Association of Chief Police Officers All chief officers from Home Office police forces and the chief officers of the Police Service for Northern Ireland belong to ACPO. It is a professional body and provides many different advisory committees (e.g. on firearms, training and crime) and contributes to debates on important issues such as drugs, policies and sex offenders.

ACPOS Same as ACPO but for Scotland.

APA Association of Police Authorities.

BPA Black Police Association. Provides support and advice for all police officers and managers in relation to issues of ethnicity and race. There is a national BPA, as well as a growing number of force BPAs.

CPS Crown Prosecution Service. The CPS acts as the prosecuting agency for the police and most cases need authorisation in order to progress to court.

GPA Gay Police Association. Provides support and advice for all police officers and managers in relation to relevant issues.

HMIC Her Majesty's Inspectorate of Constabulary. A body of senior people (some of them retired Chief Constables) appointed by the Crown who inspect police forces and publish reports on what they find. There is a Chief Inspector of Constabulary who oversees the work of regional offices.

IPCC Independent Police Complaints Commission.

NPIA National Police Improvement Agency.

Police Federation Like the police officers' trade union (at least for officers of the ranks from constable up to Chief Inspector). Set up under an Act of Parliament, the Federation has regional offices across England and Wales and a national office in Surrey. Each force has a number of Federation representatives who are elected by its members. They will provide advice on aspects of welfare, conditions of service, discipline and health and safety.

SOCA Serious and Organised Crime Agency.

Superintendents' Association Similar to the Federation but for Superintendents and Chief Superintendents.

Common Abbreviations and Jargon

ABH Actual bodily harm—an offence under section 47 of the Offences Against the Person Act 1861. Generally involves a fairly high degree of injury like lost tooth and bad bruising. See also section 47 and OAP.

ACC Assistant Chief Constable.

AFIS Automated fingerprint identification system.

Airwave Digital radio system used by all officers and forces.

ANPR Automated Number Plate Recognition system.

Appropriate adult Every person under 17 who is in custody and being interviewed requires the assistance of an appropriate adult. Usually a parent or guardian but not necessarily. Also required by other vulnerable people in custody such as people with mental difficulties.

APS Acting police sergeant. Applies to other ranks as well, e.g. A/CI = acting Chief Inspector.

ARV Armed response vehicle.

ASBO Anti-social behaviour order. Order passed by the courts to stop people whose behaviour is making their neighbours' lives miserable. The police and local authority can apply for them.

BCU Basic command unit.

Brief A lawyer representing a defendant.

C & D Complaints and discipline department. Now more usually known as Professional Standards Department or PSD (see below).

CDRP Crime and Disorder Reduction Partnership—set up under the Crime and Disorder Act 1998.

CHIS Covert human intelligence source (informant).

CJSU Criminal justice support unit. Department responsible for managing proposed prosecution files and related matters. See also CJU.

CJU Criminal justice unit—same as CJSU.

Club number See CRO number.

Con & Use The Road Vehicles (Construction and Use) Regulations. Amended frequently and containing masses of useful detail about vehicles such as how much tread they have to have on their tyres and what sort of condition they have to be in, and less useful bits such as the requirements of motorised hedge trimmers and whether trailers carrying timber are exempt from having mud-flaps.

CRO number Criminal Records Office number. Every convicted person is allocated one of these. Recorded on PNC. See also Club number.

D & C Discipline and complaints department—now more usually known as Professional Standards Department or PSD (see below)

D & D Drunk and disorderly. The offence committed where someone is disorderly while drunk in a public place.

Dep/DCC Deputy Chief Constable

DNA Deoxyribonucleic acid (see why it's just called DNA?). Gene identification. Found in hair, semen and other samples that are taken from suspects or recovered from crime scenes.

DPA Data Protection Act.

Due care Driving without due care and attention. Probably the most common motoring offence. Includes everything from ignoring road signs to driving through puddles and splashing pedestrians.

Egress Normally used in crime reports to refer to the way a criminal got out of a building. Egress is the opposite of 'entry' and often criminals use a different way out from the way they got in.

FPN Fixed Penalty Notice.

FPND Fixed Penalty Notice for Disorder—may be issued for certain offences such as section 5 (see below).

Guv'nor Inspector (term used in London and southern forces).

HORT/1 Home Office Road Traffic 1 form—also known as a producer, this is the piece of paper that officers give to motorists allowing them seven days to produce their driving documents at a police station of their choice.

IO Investigation officer.

IP Injured party or person (victim).

MFH Missing from home.

MO Modus operandi. The method of operating used by a particular criminal (e.g. always wears a mask, kicks in kitchen door).

MOP Member of the public.

NFA 'No further action' (method of writing off police calls or tasks) or 'no fixed abode'.

Nick Police Station.

NIM National Intelligence Model.

NIP Notice of Intended Prosecution. Notice (oral or in writing) that you have to give motorists within 14 days before reporting them for certain road traffic offences (such as speeding) unless they have had an accident at the time.

OAP Offences Against the Person Act 1861.

OPL Over the prescribed limit (driving whilst . . .).

PI Participating informant—person (non-police) who has been authorised to play a limited part in criminal activity in order to catch offenders.

PII Public interest immunity—legal expression whereby the police and others apply to a court to prevent documents or other evidence from being used, usually because it would pose a threat to public interest (e.g. because an informant is named in the document).

PNC Police National Computer. Contains details of all people with criminal convictions, etc. See also CRO number.

PSD Professional Standards Department—the people who deal with discipline and complaints against police officers.

PSU Police support unit.

Section 4 Offence of putting person in fear of unlawful violence (Public Order Act 1986).

Section 5 Offence of using threatening, abusive or insulting words or behaviour (Public Order Act 1986).

Section 29 production Power to allow prisoners out of custody so that they can help the police with enquiries into other offences. Taken from section 29 of the Criminal Justice Act 1961.

Section 47 See also ABH and OAP.

Section 136 The power to remove people from public places if they appear to be suffering from a mental disorder. Taken from the Mental Health Act 1983.

SIO Senior investigating officer.

Skipper Sergeant (usually heard in South East England).

SOCO Scenes of crime officer.

Super Superintendent

TDA Offence of 'taking and driving away' (Theft Act 1968, section 12). Referred to in newspapers as 'joy riding'. See also UTMV, TWOC and TWLA.

TWLA Offence of 'taking without lawful authority' (Theft Act 1968, section 12).

TWOC Offence of taking conveyance without the owner's consent (Theft Act 1968, section 12).

UTMV Offence of unlawful taking of motor vehicle (Theft Act 1968, section 12).

Appendix 2

THE PHONETIC ALPHABET

A great deal of police communication is done via the radio network. The network is now digital and gives a much higher quality of reception than anything the police have experienced before. Despite the high quality it is essential that when passing a message an officer does so as accurately as possible, and the area that has the greatest capacity for mistakes is when giving a name, address or vehicle registration number. For this reason the police use the standard phonetic alphabet in which each letter has an associated word. If you do join the police service you will need to know this alphabet, and it is worth learning it sooner rather than later (not only that, but it does crop up in the occasional pub quiz).

The standard alphabet used by the UK police, emergency services and armed forces is as follows:

A	Alpha	H	Hotel	O	Oscar	U	Uniform
B	Bravo	I	India	P	Papa	V	Victor
C	Charlie	J	Juliet	Q	Quebec	W	Whiskey
D	Delta	K	Kilo	R	Romeo	X	X-ray
E	Echo	L	Lima	S	Sierra	Y	Yankee
F	Foxtrot	M	Mike	T	Tango	Z	Zulu
G	Golf	N	November				

The Irish spelling of 'Whiskey' is deliberate, but not compulsory.

Index

LAW FROM OXFORD

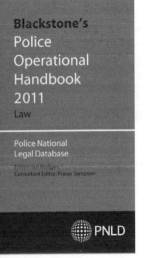

Blackstone's Police Operational Handbook 2011: Law

Police National Legal Database (PNLD)
Editor: **Ian Bridges**, Legal Adviser, PNLD
Consultant Editor: **Fraser Sampson**, Chief
Executive, West Yorkshire Police Authority

*"Easy to find legislation with highlighted notes
assisting with fast decision making"*
        Sergeant Grey Cooney, Metropolitan Police

• Portable, succinct reference for police officers on the beat

• Covers over 100 different offences in the areas of
general crime, assaults, drugs, sexual offences, public
disorder, firearms, licensing and road traffic

November 2010 | 916 Pages | 978-0-19-959519-8

Oxford University Press law books are available from your
regular supplier, or visit **www.oup.com/uk/policing**

LAW FROM OXFORD

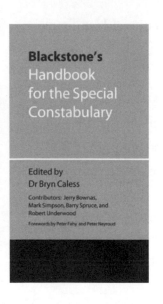

Blackstone's Handbook for the Special Constabulary

Edited by **Bryn Caless**
Barry Spruce, **Jerry Bownas**, **Robert Underwood**, and **Mark Simpson**

• The only dedicated, up-to-date publication aimed at Specials

• Structured around those areas of policing indentified in the National Strategy for the Special Constabulary 2008

• Includes coverage of police powers, criminal law, crime scene management, and neighbourhood policing

480 pages | 978-0-19-959257-9 | July 2010